166 Ways to Dramatically Increase the Value of Your Home

In a Competitive Real Estate Market

166 Ways to Dramatically Increase the Value of Your Home

In a Competitive Real Estate Market

1st Edition

By

Joshua Fant

North Pacific Publishing
Seattle, WA

ISBN 978-0-9742691-1-5

About the Author

Joshua Fant is the owner of a successful real estate brokerage in the State of Washington which handles both real estate sales and property management consisting of single family homes and apartment buildings. He is also an avid real estate investor with various real estate holdings.

He began investing in single family real estate in 2001 specializing in buying houses that required some renovation. By purchasing homes that needed some work, he knew that he could purchase for a discount and drive up the value by making improvements to the properties. Joshua oversaw the improvements on the properties by designing and managing the remodeling process himself. He unlocked potential cash flow from homes that most people overlooked by not only improving their livability, but by also adding additional livable units when possible. He has a unique talent for turning distressed properties into cash flowing properties.

While remodeling and managing his own growing portfolio of properties, Mr. Fant became a licensed mortgage loan broker to further his knowledge of real estate financing and to develop relationships in the finance industry.

In early 2008, Joshua developed a property management company called North Pacific Properties, LLC to begin managing properties for other people in addition to his own. Successfully managing his own properties for 8 years and originating over 250 real estate loans prepared him to successfully manage multiple rentals properties and screen applicants with an underwriter's touch while generating huge profits for himself and his clients.

Today North Pacific Properties continues to grow at a rapid rate in the Pacific Northwest United States with revenues doubling each year. The company is a leading competitor in both property management and real estate sales. In addition to the real estate sales and property management of North Pacific Properties, Mr. Fant created and operates a maintenance and repair company to facilitate improvements on his and his clients' homes as needed.

Table of Contents Summary

                              High Return on investment

                              Moderate Return on investment

                              Low Return on investment

                          $2,000 - $7,999

                              High Return on investment

                              Moderate Return on investment

                              Low Return on investment

                          $0 - $1,999

                              High Return on investment

                              Moderate Return on investment

                              Low Return on investment

              Table 2   **Exterior Improvements**

                          Greater than $8,000

                              High Return on investment

                              Moderate Return on investment

                              Low Return on investment

                          $2,000 - $7,999

                              High Return on Investment

                              Moderate Return on Investment

                              Low Return on Investment

$0 - $1,999

High Return on investment
Moderate Return on investment
Low Return on investment

Table of Contents

Introduction

This book is intended for those whom are considering selling their home in the near future and seeking ideas to maximize their sales value, and for those seeking ideas to improve their home for their own enjoyment while increasing future sales value. Whichever is the case, the inspirations in this book will yield a positive outcome if put to action. The book is loaded with 166 great ideas on improving your home and its value. The book includes 100 ideas for improving the interior of your home plus another 66 ideas for improving the exterior and surroundings. At the end of this book after you have read all of the ways you can improve your home, I have compiled the ideas into different categories to help you plan your improvements based on cost and return on investment.

There are multiple factors that affect the value of your home: structural improvements, perception & presentation, safety, function and comfort. Whether an improvement is structural or simply makes the house more presentable, various types of improvements, large and small, can have a positive effect on the value of your property and people's perception of value.

A few tips moving forward:

There will be some slight repetition in this book as I offer a variety options for the reader to explore and spruce up their home and add value at different price points. For example, I have an improvement titled 'install under-cabinet lighting in the kitchen' in one area of the book and later mention a complete kitchen remodel which includes under cabinet lighting. One of these improvements will cost approximately $100 for people seeking inexpensive improvements while the later improvement can cost upwards of $30,000 for those seeking more extreme forms of improvements.

The book is meant to feed your brain with a multitude of ideas, both expensive and inexpensive for improving your home. After reading through the book, you will have the tools to develop a general idea of the different items you will improve based on cost, time and resources you have. Your plan may include a combination of some small items and some large items to complete improvements that meet a specific budget and which result in the greatest return on investment.

The ideas and improvements in this book will not improve the value of your home unless they are done well. In fact, if these ideas are done poorly, they can actually decrease the value of your home whether you are painting a single room or performing a complete kitchen remodel.

While you may be able to handle most of the improvements in this book, you should strongly consider hiring a tradesman to be sure improvements are done well and someone is accountable. If you can afford to have someone else do the work, below are some tips to hiring a contractor or handyman:

- Do not ever pay 100% upfront
- Always get receipts for materials and for complete job
- Ask about a warranty or guarantee
- If you are uncomfortable paying for supplies upfront, meet the handyman or contractor at the store and pay for the materials yourself
- Do not automatically go with the lowest bidder. There may be a reason the lowest bidder is inexpensive.

Thank you for buying this book. I truly hope you gain some knowledge and helpful ideas which will result in a surprisingly positive return on your money and sales value.

Section 1

Interior Improvements

Update the kitchen Cabinets: Paint, Refinish, Reface or Replace

There are multiple ways to spruce up the kitchen cabinetry. Whether you only spend a little bit of money to paint them or go all out and replace the cabinets, all of the options below can improve the look of the cabinets:

Paint the cabinets

Painting the cabinets is a common fix if your cabinets are already painted or if the existing cabinets are made of a dark wood product that makes your kitchen feel like a cave. Regardless, painted cabinets can be really nice if done with care. It is not required, but it's best to remove the cabinet doors and hardware so you can properly prepare the doors for painting. You do not have to sand the paint off, but you do need to give a light sanding to the cabinet faces and doors to create a rough service for your paint to adhere too. Because the cabinets need to be easily cleanable during use, you should choose a strong gloss paint that can be wiped clean often. Also be sure to choose a light color, using this opportunity to brighten up your kitchen. After you have primed and painted the cabinets and they have fully dried, re-hang the doors and apply the hardware. Repainting the cabinets is a quick and inexpensive way to provide a bright and fresh facelift to the kitchen.

Reface the cabinets

Another method growing in popularity to upgrade old cabinets is cabinet refacing. Old doors, side panels and drawer fronts are replaced with new doors and drawer fronts. Matching veneer is bonded to casework. Refacing can be done in a wide variety of wood types, colors and door styles, producing the look of brand new cabinets in about a week, without tearing out the old boxes. Refacing cabinets is something that you hire a company to do. Because you have to hire a professional to reface your cabinets, the cost will be higher. It is recommended to get multiple bids and decide for yourself if this is a route you want to pursue. The end result can be superb and you don't have to get dirty, but the cost could be a factor in deciding to go this route.

Refinish the cabinets

If your cabinets are made of quality wood and have never been painted (or they have been painted and you don't mind stripping the paint off with chemicals), refinishing the cabinets can be a very nice and price conscious improvement. To do this properly, you will want to remove the doors from the cabinets and all the hardware (hinges, handles, bumpers, etc.). Sand the cabinets and both sides of all the doors using the different grades of sandpaper until you have bare or almost bare wood. (Be careful not to sand through the top thin layer of nice wood known as wood veneer.) At this point you may choose to put a clear finish over the cabinet faces and doors or if you are feeling brave, you can choose a stain and refinish them to a specific color. If you did not get all of the original finish off of the wood, staining the cabinet a new color may not be a wise choice because the stain may not absorb into or penetrate the wood evenly. Follow the instructions on your wood products to finish refinishing the doors and cabinet faces. Re-apply all the hardware and hang the doors to see the finished product.

New cabinets

The most expensive method to upgrading your kitchen cabinetry is to replace your cabinets. For some of you, your cabinets may be too far gone to refinish, reface or paint. Replacing your cabinets may be the only option to give your kitchen the facelift it needs. Time to get bids. Contractors are tripping over themselves to get your business. Call around and get quotes for new cabinets. Depending upon where you live, you may have access to stores that sell cabinets that you can install yourself.

Update Kitchen Countertops

If your kitchen has outdated laminate, wood, tile or synthetic countertops you should seriously consider new countertops. There are various types of countertops you can choose from to replace your existing counters. If you are going to replace your countertops, hire professional installers because the finished product needs to be perfect.

Below I will mention the most common types of countertops in an effort to educate you on the different varieties. For the purpose of appealing to the largest audience of buyers, I recommend going with a stone countertop:

Laminate

Laminate countertops are typically made of particle board or plywood and have a hard plastic veneer made to look like something else (stone, marble, solid colors, etc.). There are some decent laminate countertops available on the market for the budget conscious, but these countertops are meant for the do-it-yourselfer and not as nice as stone.

Tile

Tile countertops can be done with any sort of ceramic or stone tile. Tile countertops are usually done in lieu of granite countertops because they can be done on a budget, while providing the illusion of stone. The downside is that the grout lines between the tiles are germ and dirt collectors. I would never want a tile countertop in my house for this reason. I think it is a bad idea and every time I see one I can see food and dried colored sauces in the grout lines. Builders will install tile countertops to keep costs down and sell their houses quickly. The reason they do this is because they can get a tile guy to give them a bid on tiling the bathroom, fireplace and kitchen countertops and be done with the house by the time the tile guy is finished with his job. No need for professional countertops when you have a tile guy right already working in the house right?

Corian

Corian is a synthetic (man-made) manufactured countertop product that is usually sold by large home improvement stores. It is a plastic like substance that comes in multiple colors and can be custom made to fit your kitchen. It is a very pedestrian product, but still better than laminate or tile countertops in my opinion because of its custom and seamless installation. I would never use it myself. In my personal opinion, Corian is an outdated product and unflattering. Most people desire stone slabs on their countertops. If you are trying to impress buyers, do not install a countertop that most people will have to tear out and start over again.

Granite

Granite is the most common countertop product and while it is not that expensive, it is a huge step up from laminate, tile or Corian countertops. Granite comes in a huge variety of colors and types from around the world. If you shop around enough, you might be able to get your granite plus installation for anywhere between $1200-$2000 complete. Many people will quote $4000-$6000 to install granite countertops. If you shop around enough, you will be able to cut those numbers in half because granite is not that expensive. Once you install large solid slabs of stone into your kitchen, it will transform the look and feel of your entire house. The downside of granite is that it typically has to be installed professionally and the cost might be over your budget. The other downside is that it can be porous, but I have personally never seen a bad stain in granite.

Marble

Marble is a gorgeous stone and common in many high-end homes. It is very costly as well. Besides the cost, the stone can be scratched, chipped and cracked as it is not as hard as some other stones. Marble countertops are typically white with gray lines.

Quartz / Silestone

Gaining popularity are Quartz countertops. Quartz countertops are a great product and very similar to granite, except that it is typically engineered as opposed to granite which is simply cut from the earth and polished. Quartz countertop slabs are made up of ground up quartz and built so strong and solid they are nonporous. Silestone is a common type of quartz slab. The color choices are superb and contemporary. The slabs are durable and smooth. It resists scratch, stains and heat for the most part. If you do scratch it, the scratches can be buffed out. Quartz or Silestone is a great countertop and while its price is about equal to granite, it is a more solid product.

Concrete

Concrete countertops can be very nice and modern if done well. Doing them well is the key or the end result will be a countertop with rough uneven edges or poor coloration. The great thing about concrete countertops is that you can customize the shape, color and texture. You can add colored glass or other items to create a border or make an artistic statement. You can also purchase different colored dyes to produce a countertop to match your kitchen color scheme. Once the concrete countertop has been poured into its form and dried solid, the surface needs to be treated with a coating to make it smooth and glossy like granite. At this point, the countertop can look spectacular. I recommend that you have a professional do it. One thing to note is that by the time you pay a professional to create the concrete countertop and install it, you could have had granite professionally installed, which will be more widely accepted among buyers. Concrete is a way to create a great looking and modern stone countertop on a budget if you can pull it off yourself.

Soapstone

Soapstone is a beautiful stone that has an emerald tone to it. I installed it into a home once, but I would never do it again. Soapstone is very porous and needs to be oiled weekly to stay dark and shiny keeping its beautiful color. Otherwise, the stone looks dull. I was trying to sell the house that I installed the soapstone in and it seemed like every time I visit the house I had to apply mineral oil to it because it kept absorbing it. I regretted putting it in the house and felt guilty that the buyers of the house were going to have to upkeep the countertop like a living creature. It was a beautiful stone, but very expensive and high maintenance.

Improve Kitchen Lighting

A well lit kitchen is crucial being that the kitchen is the most important room in the entire house. Whether someone is an experienced cook or average kitchen user, a bright functional kitchen will be important to all. Since your food comes from the kitchen, you want it to be well lit to be sure you are eating good clean food and after you clean up, you want to be sure you got all of the crumbs and cooking debris. A few ways to light up your kitchen are with under cabinet lighting, recessed lights above the countertops, pendent lights, lights in the cabinets, working bulbs in your oven hood, sconces and ceiling lights.

Under cabinet lighting has been mentioned a few times in this book because they serve as a function and add drama to your kitchen. Under cabinet lighting comes in fluorescent or halogen. Fluorescent lights use less electricity and have evolved quite a bit in the quality of light they emit. Halogen lights are very nice and bright; however they use a lot of electricity and can become dangerously hot.

Recessed / Can lights are great in a kitchen for directing light right onto the workspaces. There is an art to positioning the recessed lights in the ceiling so that the light hits the counter tops properly. For example, if you install the lights too close to the center of the kitchen, then your head might cast a shadow on the countertops. If you if install them too close to the border of the kitchen ceiling, the lights could be blocked by the upper cabinets.

Pendent lights and sconces are great lights to add some design components to your kitchen. Pendent lights can be great additions above a kitchen island or bar. Sconces can be make a perfect touch to add some light to a wall or entry way.

A not-so-common source of light is in-cabinet lighting. In-cabinet lighting is typically used when there are cabinets with see-through glass doors. If the inside of the cabinet is tidy with plates, bowls and/or glasses perfectly lined up, lights inside can add some dimension to the kitchen. However, keeping a cabinet tidy may not be that easy, so lighting it up to showcase the interior may be a bad decision.

Kitchen Island

The search for more storage space and countertops in the kitchen never ends. If you have a large kitchen and think you can squeeze an island into it without creating a cluttered space, then jump on this opportunity to add a kitchen island. Kitchen islands can be custom built or purchased at home stores.

Custom built kitchen islands on a budget

A kitchen island can be built on a budget if you want to simply create some more counter space. Be careful with the budget route because doing something improperly will take away from your value. However, if you are confident that you can make this look good, one way to do this is to purchase the metal conduit piping that screws together at the local home improvement or hardware store to create your legs. Cut a piece of plywood just shy of the size of the counter top that you want. Now that you have your foundation, you can find a local metal fabricator to make you a stainless steel top with finished sides. Another option for a top is to purchase a large chopping block and have cut to size. Stores like IKEA sell various lengths of chopping block countertops that can be purchased and screwed right to the legs. Some people will use antique furniture and change the top to a chopping block or piece of stone. The possibilities are endless.

High-end custom built kitchen island

The most recommended kitchen island would be one that matches your existing kitchen cabinetry. If you can purchase the same cabinets and fronts that match your current cabinets and top off with the same countertop, this would be a great addition to the kitchen. Be sure to leave plenty of space for people to move about the kitchen if you decide to build and install a custom kitchen island.

Buy a kitchen island

The simplest way to add a kitchen island is to purchase one at a store. These prefabricated islands are great because they fit the budget and come in multiple shapes and sizes. You will have trouble finding one that is an exact match to your kitchen, but for the cost of $300-$1000, a perfect match will not matter. A store bought kitchen island is barely an improvement to your home because it is not attached to the property. It really falls under the category of staging. Sometimes you can find used antique kitchen islands as well which may add a little more character to your space.

Upgrade Appliances

Appliances are important to a well functioning home. While appliances perform important functions in the home, they also serve as centerpieces to complete a well designed home.

Function

Every home needs a properly working oven, refrigerator, washing machine, dryer and sometimes dishwasher. If you have all of these appliances, be sure they are all in good working order before you list. Appliances should be clean and ready for their next job with properly tightened handles, clean and safe.

Aesthetics

Over the years, appliances have been a growing attraction in the home. High-end appliances lure in buyers with their commercial and pricey appeal. In the last decade, stainless steel appliances have grown in popularity beyond what anyone would have imagined outside of a commercial kitchen. Stainless appliances are in high demand and have an definite effect over the perception of your kitchen. If you currently have mixed colored appliances, or old white appliances, almond, green, red, etc., you may want to consider replacing all of the appliances with stainless steel appliances. Even better is if you can get all of the appliances by the same brand and product line. By staying with one company and product line, you can ensure that all of the appliances look very similar with the same handles and finish. Replacing all of your kitchen appliances with a moderate brand of stainless appliances can be done for less than $5000. If you want to replace the appliances with higher-end brands, you could exceed $15000.

You don't have to replace your appliances with stainless steel appliances to make your kitchen look ten times better. As I mentioned above, you may currently have a mix of colors or brands in your kitchen. You could replace all of the appliances to one single color and brand. For example, all white appliances or all black appliances look nice too; especially when they are brand new.

Laundry room appliances have been getting better and better over the years. Just as kitchen appliances have become more commercial looking, so have washers and dryers. More and more people are purchasing front load washers and dryers. These machines can be stacked to save space or set side by side. Washer and dryer sets come in all sorts of colors. Most people go with white, but you can get stainless, gray, black, red, blue, etc. A new matching set of laundry equipment will really impress and can be purchases at appliance or local home improvement stores.

In the end, appliances can cost a lot of money to replace, but the improvement can be quick and effective. Buyers do not want to buy a house and then turn around and spend over $1,000 to replace an appliance. Most buyers demand a turn-key house. After a buyer spends all of their cash on the down payment to buy your house, they will not be able to afford appliances and other large ticket items. Therefore, the more you spend in advance to make your home more turn-key, the more attractive your house becomes to the general buying public.

Upgrade Plumbing Fixtures in the Kitchen

A fast way to spruce up any kitchen is to upgrade and replace the plumbing fixtures. If you have standard or low grade fixtures, or your fixtures are over seven years old, you may want to consider upgrading and replacing them.

A few key factors to consider when determining whether to upgrade your fixtures include the brand of the fixture, its functionality & style and the finish.

Brand

The brand of your faucet can be very telling. There are inexpensive budget brands that have cheap parts inside and do not hold up over time. If you have an inexpensive rental grade faucet, then perhaps you should consider upgrading to a better brand. People who spend a lot of time in the kitchen will notice if you have a cheap faucet. The cost to replace a faucet with a more expensive one can range from $125.00 to $1,000 depending upon how fancy you want to make it.

Functionality & Style

The functionality and style will also affect the price of your new faucet quite a bit. For example, you have the choice of a single handle faucet versus a double (hot and cold) handle faucet. You also have to decide if you want a sprayer hose attachment. The sprayer hoses are sometimes separate from the faucet assembly and are mounted on the sink in a 4th hole. Or you can get faucets where the spray attachment is the actual faucet head and it simply removes to spray and slides back into place. Another stylistic feature of kitchen faucets which are very popular and affordable are the tall single handle commercial kitchen faucets with the spray head that hangs down high above the sink.

Finish

Another feature of kitchen faucets that you have to decide on is the finish. What finish will look the best in your kitchen? There are a multitude of finish options available today. Just a few options are chrome, stainless steel, oil rubbed bronze, bronze, brushed nickel, brass, white and black. The most affordable are typically the chrome faucets. There is really no reason to get anything besides chrome or stainless as long as it matches the rest of the hardware in the kitchen. Chrome would not be your best option if you have oil rubbed bronze handles on your kitchen cabinets. In this case you should install an oil rubbed bronze faucet. As fancy as this sounds, oil rubbed bronze will not be much more expensive than chrome. However, there are less options with the custom colors, so you may be limited to higher prices because you are limited to selection versus chrome which comes in all price points to match your pocket book. Chrome should work in any situation.

Fresh Kitchen Paint

Repainting the kitchen is a quick and inexpensive way to improve one of the most important rooms in a house. Paint the kitchen with bright neutral tones to open up the space. If you already have bright neutral toned walls, then you can skip this step. In many cases, people have been known to experiment with fun colors to customize the kitchen to their liking. When it comes times to sell, we must remove our personality from the house and neutralize every room one by one. If you only repaint one room in the entire house, I recommend the kitchen because it is the focal point. Be sure to use a gloss or semi-gloss paint so that it can be easily wiped off (unless your walls are not completely smooth in which case you would want to use a matte finish to hide the imperfections). In fact, I am going to contradict myself here. If you are selling the home, walls always look better with a matte paint (no shine or gloss). However, you cannot easily clean or wipe dirt off of matte walls. If you intend to live in the house for over a year, I would not recommend a matte finish unless you intend on applying another coat when you list your house. Matte is great for hiding imperfections in walls, but its roughness attracts dirt.

Upgrade Kitchen Flooring

Not all vinyl flooring is bad. In fact, they make some pretty good vinyl flooring these days. However, if you are one of the many people who have the sad old vinyl flooring that is 25 years old with bent corners and fragments missing, then you have to consider a new floor.

Vinyl to vinyl

Vinyl is inexpensive to both purchase and install. If you are on a tight budget, but your vinyl floor definitely needs to be replaced, then measure your floor and head to the nearest flooring store to price out a vinyl that will match the current color scheme of your kitchen. Remember to keep it neutral. Get some bids for installation. Flooring stores will usually offer up bids to install the flooring for you. If you floor is small enough, you can probably purchase a fragment roll large enough to cover at a great discount.

Vinyl to tile

Tile floors in a kitchen are so nice because of the ability to stand up to water, tearing, staining and other sorts of damage common with other types of flooring. Not only is tile a strong alternative to other flooring, it can be a stunning improvement to any kitchen. Tiling your kitchen floor is a great investment to improve the best room in the house, but it can be costly depending upon who you hire to install it and the type of tile you choose. Ceramic tile will be a lot less expensive than a natural stone such as granite, slate or marble.

Install Under-Cabinet Lighting

Under cabinet lighting is a great addition to any kitchen. Lighting the countertops makes the kitchen much more functional and enjoyable. There are a few options for under cabinet lighting that can affect the cost. Your options for under cabinet lighting are halogen lighting or fluorescent.

Fluorescent under cabinet lighting

Fluorescent under cabinet lighting used to be large and cumbersome with cords visible. Florescent lighting has actually come a long way, will last longer than halogen and uses less electricity. If you want dimmers on your under cabinet lights, you will have to go with Halogen.

Halogen under cabinet lights

Halogen lights are brighter, have a better color and will dim. I noticed that with my halogen under cabinet lights, I have to replace the bulbs often. The bulbs are almost $6.00 each, so this gets frustrating when you are replacing a bulb per month. I think it is because I have them on a dimmer and it puts stress on the bulbs.

My suggestion for installing or replacing under cabinet lighting it to make hiding the power cords your priority. If you can recess your wiring into the walls or behind the cabinet, that is best. The least expensive route is to install some new fluorescent lights beneath the cabinets that tie together in a series and plug into the outlet. There is no light switch when you go this route. You turn them on and off right on the units themselves.

For a little bit more money, you should have an electrician install a light switch for you and bury the electrical wires in the wall so you cannot see anything but lights. And if you are going to have an electrician bury your wires and give you a light switch, then you should go a step further and have the halogen lights installed versus the florescent lights. The halogen lights do not cost much more than the modern florescent lights. They are close to the same price, but they require being hardwired into your electrical system versus the ease of installation of the florescent lights which can simply be plugged into the wall.

Create a Breakfast Nook Area

A breakfast nook is a home attribute growing in popularity as modern families are continuously on the go from morning to night. Whether large or small, a breakfast nook makes a great addition to a kitchen. A breakfast nook can be large or small. If you have room in your kitchen to create a breakfast nook, you should try to create it while preserving as much sense of space as you can. Do not try to squeeze a four top table into a small area. A breakfast nook can be a small two topper table with 2 chairs. The nook can be put into a corner. Many breakfast nooks have benches built into the wall that can also be used as additional storage.

Whether you are getting children off to school in the morning or enjoying your first cup of coffee with the morning paper (or your tablet), a nook will serve as a highly popular feature of your home sure to impress potential buyers.

Add a Kitchen Pantry

A pantry is a room where food, provisions, dishes, or linens are stored. The pantry is typically a room off of the kitchen that contains shelving and cabinetry to hold all of these goods. Additional storage space in a kitchen is an overlooked feature with huge functionality. The kitchen pantry is becoming a sought-after feature in many homes. Having the ability to store large amounts of food and various kitchen products such as garbage bags, paper towels and cleaning supplies is a money saving benefit for you and potential buyers since many of these items can be purchased for a lower cost in bulk.

Does your home have a kitchen pantry? If not, examine the kitchen to see if you can create a kitchen pantry. There are a few different pantry types: A walk in pantry, a built in pantry and a piece of furniture that serves as a pantry.

A walk-in pantry

Large walk-in pantries come standard in high-end homes with large kitchens. Unfortunately, for the average or older home, pantries are not as common. Space was tight and they were not deemed a priority even though the need to store bulk items would be needed more in the average to low income home. A walk in pantry is the best pantry one can have. A walk in pantry consists of a large room with lots of shelving, tall ceilings and room for everything including the mop. Creating a walk in pantry will have the greatest effect on the value. A walk in pantry can be created out of extra space in an over sized kitchen, or a nearby closet that you thought was only meant for coats and boots.

Other types of pantries may not be attached to the kitchen, but close by. Some are tucked in an alcove off the kitchen or dining room or configured into a small hallway or under a staircase

Built-in pantry

Rather than going through the expense of a walk in pantry or sacrifice of space, many homeowners find that they can build cabinets into walls. If you refrigerator is wrapped like a kitchen cabinet, you may consider building a cabinet with the same materials alongside the fridge will pull out shelving for extra storage items. Another way this could be done is a flush mount cabinet as long as you have a one to two feet of empty space in your walls or a room that is hardly used behind the wall that could stand to lose a foot of space. The flush mount built in pantry is a great way to add storage to your kitchen without sacrificing kitchen square footage. I don't recommend this, but one time I removed an entire chimney in an old house from above the roof line, all the way down to the basement. I did this to open up the extra square feet in the walls in both the kitchen and second floor. The chimney was not being used any more, and while the removal created a lot of dust, it was surprisingly easy how the bricks came apart. I put an ad on craigslist for free bricks and they were all gone within 24 hours because people desire old red bricks. Doing something like this opens up enough space in a well to create a large pantry.

A piece of furniture used as storage

If you do not have the room to create a walk in pantry, but enough space for a piece of furniture, consider a hutch or cabinet of some sort. Hutches come in all different shapes and sizes. If you look hard enough, you can find the perfect hutch to match your kitchen. You can use the drawers for dried foods, paper towels, big dishes, etc. Keep an open mind when seeking out furniture for your kitchen. You can find an inexpensive piece of furniture used online for $100, repaint it to match your kitchen and all of the sudden you have custom kitchen cabinetry.

Complete Kitchen Remodel: Flooring, Cabinets, Fixtures, Lighting and Countertops

The kitchen is commonly known to be the room that has the upmost importance in a home and has the greatest return on investment. A beautiful, well appointed kitchen can be the difference between a quick sale of a home at asking price or higher, versus a home that sits on the market with little or no bites.

Adding an addition or dormer to the home and increasing its square feet is the biggest improvement you can make to increase the value of your home. However, if you want to increase the value with the space you already have, the kitchen should be your focus. The average return on investment for a kitchen remodel ranges from about 80 percent to 90 percent. A complete kitchen remodel will cost $12,000 to $35,000+. A complete kitchen remodel means you will be replacing cabinets, countertops, lighting appliances, plumbing fixtures and flooring.

In other sections of this book, I go into detail about the individual improvements you can make in your kitchen such as replacing cabinets, countertops, lighting, appliances, plumbing fixtures and hardware. The overall kitchen remodel is the best way to go to boost your home value. Below I mention a few ideas to keep in mind during your remodel in order to net the largest return on investment and increase the value of your home dramatically:

Function

The kitchen has to be as functional as possible for you, the future home owner and families. For the kitchen to be functional it must have an ergonomic layout. I urge you to learn about and keep the triangle design in mind. The triangular layout is the most efficient use of kitchen layouts. The goal of a good kitchen work triangle is to place the three most common work sites within a close distance of each other, creating an efficient work zone. The three work sites include the refrigerator, stone/oven and work area including the sink. The triangular layout and design of your kitchen creates a much better experience for preparing meals and promotes flow through the kitchen.

Some other things to add to function include making sure the door handle to the fridge is closest to you. In other words, you want the fridge door to open away from you, not towards you. Cabinet doors should also open away from you so you don't have to walk around the doors to get what's inside.

Storage and organization

When re-designing your kitchen and picking out new cabinetry, take this opportunity to create as must storage space as possible. Do your best to incorporate the right mix of storage solutions which will be important to future home owners.

Style

Make your kitchen beautiful and remember to stick with the style of your home. You have a wide array of materials and finishes to choose from starting with your flooring, to your cabinets, countertops, lighting and appliances. Do not install the least expensive products you can find. Your goal is to increase the value of your home. If you do not use high end materials for your kitchen remodel, many home buyers will be deterred by this. If a kitchen is not up to a buyers standards, then the buyers will start calculating the cost to replace all of the work you did to make it right. This cost goes against you. And since most home buyers do not want to spend any of their own money to make a house better (after spending hundreds of thousands to buy it), chances are good that they will completely pass on your house if your remodel is not up to par.

Create a great place for entertaining and interaction

The kitchen is the place to entertain and for many, to sit and eat a quick bite before running out the door. Make sure your kitchen has space for multiple people to move about. Seating at a bar or kitchen nook is a plus. Create a kitchen where buyers will imagine themselves chatting with family members, laughing with friends or preparing a romantic meal for a loved one.

Add Bath

Adding a bathroom is always on top of the list of improvements that dramatically increase the value of a home. The lack of a bathroom is not as much of an issue in newer homes as it is in older homes. Many older homes have a single bathroom on the first floor that the entire family shares.

If your home is limited on bathrooms, I strongly recommend that you find a way to add a bathroom. Adding a bathroom does not always have to mean adding an addition to the home. Many times a bathroom can be created by cutting up a large room to create a bath or using a space that has little or no use in the house to create a useable space.

The most common place to add a bathroom is in a master bedroom or finished basement. The main floor of most houses already has a bathroom.

When adding a bathroom to the second floor of your home, it is best (for multiple reasons) to try and stack the new bathroom above the current bathroom on the first floor so you can easily tie into the plumbing of the bathroom on the first floor. Make sure the bathroom plumbing and flooring is sealed tightly so you don't have to worry about any flooding from the top floor to the main floor.

When adding a bathroom to the basement, be sure you are able to tie into the sewer line. If you find yourself below a sewer line, there is an easy fix. You will need to install a sump pump to your bathroom waste line which will pump the waste water from below grade up into the main sewer line. Adding a sump pump to eliminate bathroom waste is a little cumbersome, but it is a solution to the problem of being below the sewer line if you feel that adding the basement bathroom is going to bump up your value.

Bathtub & Shower Resurfacing

If your bathroom is in need of a makeover, but you don't want the hassle or expense of a major remodel, there is a very interesting option which I have actually done before. It is called resurfacing. Resurfacing is something that is done by a professional company. A company will come out to your home, and give you a bid to install a new acrylic bathtub liner and a matching one-piece wall system that will fit seamlessly over your existing fixtures for a brand new look. It doesn't matter what your walls look like, whether they have tile or a window. Your bathroom will look completely different and new when they are done.

If you want to skip the entire bath remodeling process and go for a quick clean look, this can usually be done in a single day. Companies that handle bath resurfacing usually do the shower enclosure and tub-to-shower conversions. You keep your current bathtub which may be almost impossible to remove without creating a lot of damage to your bathroom and the new acrylic surface fits right over it. Bathtub refinishing products are custom molded to fit over existing fixtures and can be quickly installed in one day.

As I mentioned above, I hired a company to do this for a client of mine. The home was a rental property and the owner wanted an increased rental income out of the home. I suggest a bathroom remodel because the toilet and shower were yellow and the tile on the walls was even worse. A local company came in and gave me a bid to resurface the bathtub and entire shower wall up to the ceiling. The cost was around $3,000. We replaced the flooring with new vinyl, then replaced the sink and toilet with new white porcelain. The end result was not a fancy bathroom, but a brand new, shiny, white and clean bathroom that was no longer an eye soar. I would not suggest this for a master bath because it is not a high end improvement to your home. It is just a quick and clean way to improve a very ugly bathroom.

Bathroom Porcelain Refinishing

If resurfacing your bathroom with acrylic is not for you, another great way to improve and update your bathroom is by refinishing the porcelain fixtures.

If you have an old bathtub or sink that is chipped, cracked, discolored, stained or in many cases a terrible color from the 70's, there is a solution without replacing the tub or sink. You can hire a company to refinish the porcelain. There are companies that will come out and recoat your entire bathtub or sink with a special porcelain paint that will make your fixtures look brand new again with a clean white paint. Many times in older homes you will get a green, yellow or red tub or sink. You don't have to live with this. Since you may have to break away walls and tile to remove an old cast iron bathtub, refinishing or repainting your porcelain is a much better route. You can do the sink to match and since toilets are easy to replace, you can replace the toilet for $120 to match the refinished sink and bathtub. In addition to the porcelain bathtub and sink, I have seen these same companies repaint ugly old tile in showers and baths to modernize the look and feel of the bathroom.

The cost to refinish a bathtub can range from $300 - $500. Gather estimates and go with the company you are the most comfortable with. Refinishing a bathtub is 10%-15% of the cost of hiring a company to resurface a tub or shower. And the end result is much nicer and original looking versus a shiny acrylic floor to ceiling wall which really has no style or appeal as with resurfacing.

Upgrade Bath Flooring

One sure way to give any bathroom in your house a quick facelift is by replacing the vinyl floor to a tile floor. Vinyl flooring in a bathroom can appear and feel cheap. Vinyl flooring is made to look like tile (a better type of floor), however, it curls up at the corners, tears and stains. Because a bathroom floor is typically not that large, the cost to replace the vinyl with a better floor material like tile will not be very expensive. In addition to the small size of the bath floor, the floor (versus shower surround) is a fairly easy tile job for a tile professional which will also help with costs. You will have the cost of the tile, grout and sealant plus the cost of labor for the tile installer. For an average size bathroom, you should be able to do this entire project from $650-$1000 including the cost of tearing out and throwing away the old floor. You can tile over vinyl, but sometimes this is not a great idea because the tiles and grout may eventually become loose (even if your tile professional applies a special primer down before tiling). The tile installer can screw a layer of concrete down above the vinyl floor before installing tile, but you will run into the issue of too many layers and people stubbing their toes as they enter the bathroom on the new floor which is an inch higher than the floor outside the bath.

If you have vinyl in any of your bathrooms, especially the master, you should consider replacing it with ceramic, slate, stone or marble tile to give your bathroom a huge boost in style and elegance.

Shower: Replace Shower Curtains with Glass Doors

Shower enclosures come in two basic types: Shower curtains or Glass shower doors. Deciding which type of shower enclosure to use comes down to personal preference or sometimes options are limited by the type of tub or style of home.

Shower curtains

The right shower curtain can make a bathroom look fantastic for a small amount of money. The downside is that it will make a small bathroom feel even smaller because you are essentially bringing the far bath wall 2-3 feet closer to yourself giving the illusion that the bathroom has less square footage. Shower curtains get water and soap stained in addition to mold. Shower curtains are also less desirable by most people because the liner sticks to your arm while showering. Shower curtains have an overall negative effect on a bathroom under most cases. If and when possible, I prefer clear shower glass doors.

Glass door enclosures

Glass shower doors are a great enclosure for a bathtub shower combination because they provide an open feel to the bathroom and they can help make the room feel larger. Glass door enclosures can be installed by the home owner in most cases (If your walls are tile then you might choose the assistance of a professional to avoid the potential of cracking your tile). The price for glass showers doors can range from $200.00 - $1,500. The large price variance is determined by the thickness of your glass and quality of the hardware. I recommend avoiding the frosted glass or patterned glass and sticking with clear glass which will give you the most depth perception which you want. The patterned and frosted glass will defeat the purpose of replacing your shower curtains with glass doors. You want to be able to see the back wall of the shower/bathtub giving the illusion of a larger room. If you do not want to see the back wall of the tub or shower (you want to hide it) because of some sort of flaw, then you should definitely consider the shower curtain for $20.00 or inexpensive frosted glass doors. In addition to clear glass, I also recommend glass slightly thicker than the thin stock glass doors which can be rickety and too thin. The thickness of your glass will make a large difference in your cost because it is stronger, heavier and much nicer. When ordering glass doors ask about the next thickness up and price it out. Lastly, the hardware or finish will determine your price as well. Just like your bath plumbing fixtures, you can order the trim and hardware of your glass bath enclosure in different finishes to match your bath such as: chrome, brushed nickel, oil rubbed bronze, brass and so on.

Replace Old Bath Fixtures with New Ones: Faucets, Toilet, etc.

It is crucial to have good looking and operational fixtures in your bathrooms. Look to see where you can upgrade and replace the plumbing fixtures to improve your bathroom. If you have standard or low grade fixtures, or your fixtures are over seven years old, you may want to consider upgrading and replacing them. Fixtures to consider replacing are your faucets (sinks and bath) and your toilet.

A few things to consider when upgrading fixtures are the brands, functionality/style and finish.

Faucets

The brand of your faucet can determine your replacement cost and ultimately the look of your bathroom. There are inexpensive budget brands that have cheap parts inside and won't hold up over time. If you have an inexpensive rental grade faucet, you could simply upgrade to a better brand. The cost to replace a bath faucet with a more expensive one can range from $125.00 to $800.00 depending upon how elegant or sophisticated you want to make it.

The style will also affect the price of your new faucet quite a bit. For example, you have the choice of a single handle versus a double (hot and cold) handle faucet. A contemporary or modern faucet will have its own price points leaning towards the higher end as opposed to the standard styles sold at your local home improvement store for less than $100.

The last feature of bath faucets that you have to decide on is the finish. What finish will look the best in your bathroom? There are so many options now. Just a few options are chrome, stainless steel, oil rubbed bronze, bronze, brushed nickel, brass, white and black. The most affordable are typically the chrome faucets. There is really no reason to get anything besides chrome or stainless as long as it matches the rest of the hardware/color scheme and/or tile in the bath.

The most cost effective fixtures are typically chrome. Luckily chrome looks good in almost all situations.

Toilets:

Choosing the right toilet will depend on a few things: style, manufacturer and color.

You have multiple styles to choose from. First you must decide if you want the round toilet bowl or the elongated bowl. If your bathroom is small, sometimes you are forced to install the round bowl. However, whenever possible, you should always install the elongated (oval) toilet bowl toilets. You will be pleasantly surprised by all of the other style options when you start seeking out replacement toilets. You will see multiple variations of toilet tanks. Some toilets are tankless. There are modern and contemporary toilets, as well as toilet tanks with a more classic or elegant look to them. Choose the toilet that best matches the style of your bathroom.

The manufacturer will affect your costs as well. American Standard seems to be the least expensive toilet at the home improvement stores. The next level up will be Kohler. Kohler has a great variety of styles to choose from. They have toilets with clean lines or decorative tanks. The most popular high-end toilet brand is from a Japanese company called Toto. These toilets can set you back $200 to $1000 depending on what you want it to do. A lot of times you will see Toto toilets in high end homes and in commercial applications.

New Bath Vanity

If you want to give your bathroom a facelift without the expense of remodeling the entire bathroom, you can consider just replacing the vanity. There are so many options for bathroom vanities. You can find them at home stores, home improvement stores or get creative and make a vanity out of furniture for a unique look and feel.

A new vanity can cost anywhere from $200 - $1500 depending upon where you buy it, how fancy it is and whether you have to replace the sink or pay to have it installed. Because of these factors, replacing your vanity might not be the option for you. However, if your bathroom currently has a vanity that is outdated, rotting, a bad color or style, chances are you can probably find an inexpensive replacement that will quickly increase the quality of your bathroom.

If you cannot afford to replace the vanity, then you may consider giving it a facelift by painting the existing one and replacing the handles.

The vanity is typically the centerpiece of a bathroom. Take a look at your vanity and decide whether it is something that if improved could really increase the value and quality of your bathroom.

Add a Jacuzzi Tub to Bathroom

A Jacuzzi tub is a type of bathtub that is used for recreational and relaxation purposes. Small water jets pump water into the tub to massage or comfort the user. Studies show that having a Jacuzzi bathtub in a typical home increases the value of the home. The increase in value to a home depends upon a number of characteristics of the home such as size, age, and location.

The reason that a Jacuzzi bathtub can increase the value of your home is because it is considered a structural attribute of a house. In addition to this reason, a Jacuzzi tub offers several advantages over traditional bathing facilities which cause the value of a home with a Jacuzzi to increase. A Jacuzzi is synonymous with class and status. In addition to this, owners benefit from the therapeutic value of a Jacuzzi. The benefits of Jacuzzis can vary as there are a multitude of therapeutic values that a Jacuzzi can offer different folks. Whether someone has aches and pains in their body, or uses the warm jetted water to reduce stress or relax the body before bed. Stress is a leading factor in illnesses across the world and decreasing stress can assist with immune system and longevity in the long run. Excess stress is damaging to health. It is therefore important to take time daily to relax and de-stress. The experience of the warm water of a Jacuzzi bathtubs circulating around the body is the ideal activity for to relax aching body, rejuvenate the body or assist in pain relief.

While there is no guarantee that a Jacuzzi tub installed in one of your bathrooms will increase the value of your home, it will definitely appeal to a large number of people and in almost all cases, never detract from your value. A Jacuzzi tub installed into a bathroom will improve the style of your home by creating a luxurious retreat for the homeowner to enjoy.

Replace Towel Bars in Bath

Replacing the towel bars in the bathroom is a quick and easy way to give your bathroom a facelift. Lots of varieties are available at your local home improvement store or online. Upgrade your towel bars and toilet paper roll holder from the old outdated and dingy chrome or brass plated hardware to newer, shinier more expensive Chrome or brushed nickel towel bars and holders. I have gone as far as matching all of bathroom hardware to the same finish: the towel bars to the toilet handle, toilet paper holder, bathtub stopper and towel hooks, etc. in a bathroom. Make them all match if you can and it will look great. There are even more finishes to explore including chrome, black, white, oil rubbed bronze, bronze and more. Brand new towel bars can cost you from $20.00 to over $150 each depending upon the quality and finish you choose. You may want to start this project by choosing your budget first and then working backwards from there to choose your towel bar and hardware style and finish.

Convert a Bedroom into a Bathroom

If your home needs an additional bathroom, sometimes it can be done by converting a bedroom into a bathroom. This may sound like a bad idea, but in some cases, an additional bathroom can be more important than a bedroom. If you have a house chopped up into a number of small bedrooms, but not enough bathrooms then the wise choice would be the creation of a bathroom. Choose the bedroom that is used the least or the smallest one and convert it to a bathroom.

Another possibility is to use part of an oversized bedroom to create a bathroom. You may have an oversized bedroom that could stand to lose 30 – 40 square feet. If so, you should highly consider creating a bathroom out of this extra space.

For both scenarios, you will want professional advice to be sure it is feasible to place a bathroom where you want it. In addition, you may need permits and experienced professionals to get it done well so that it undoubtedly increases the value in your home.

Will this increase the value of your home? To determine whether converting a bedroom to a bathroom will increase the value of your home, I highly suggest you consult a local real estate agent to help you with this decision before you completely remove a bedroom to create a bathroom. It may not be smart in all cases. A three bedroom house with one bathroom will in most cases be more marketable than a two bedroom two bath house because a family with two children or more would not be interested in your home any longer. A local real estate agent could tell you the different in possible give you direction on this decision.

Get Rid of Mold and Mildew in the Bathrooms and Kitchen

Mold and mildew are very common in bathrooms and kitchens along caulk lines and grout lines. Caulk and grout lines are deep corners and grooves where water gets trapped from daily usage. These locations are common in showers where the floor or top of the bathtub meets the walls. Also common in kitchens where the countertop meets the wall or backsplash. Grout can also grow mold or mildew in the grout lines. The roughness of the grout becomes a superb breeding ground for mold.

The solutions:

- Use a special cleaner to clean all of the dark mold or mildew out of the cracks, corners and crevices.
- If cleaning doesn't work, have the tile re-grouted and be sure to seal the grout afterwards to help prevent the growth
- If caulk lines are black, green or grey, remove it with a razor blade of some sort, clean the areas and re-caulk.

Re-caulking your bath and kitchen can be a very good idea. Caulk is not very expensive and no matter where you look, you can always find discolored caulk and caulk that is falling apart somewhere in your home. Do yourself a favor and re-caulk these areas to help refine the look of your home.

Complete Bath Remodel: Flooring, Bath Fixtures, Vanity, Lighting and other Amenities

A complete bathroom remodel is a great way to increase the value of your house. Important factors to consider when remodeling your bathroom to really increase your home's value are to upgrade the functionality and/or style of the bathroom.

Functionality

How can you change the functionality of a bathroom to increase your home value? First you must consider if the current layout of the bathroom is the best use of space. Is the shower in the best spot? Can the toilet be moved to create more room by the vanity? How can your bathroom layout change to make the bathroom better? The layout and functionality will also be determined by the bathroom's use. If you are remodeling a master bathroom, then you may want to add a dual vanity, jetted tub and/or glass shower enclosure. However, if you are remodeling a common bathroom, you will have a single sink with more emphasis on the vanity, flooring and toilet placement with less on the shower or bath.

A bathroom needs to have breathing room and space. If your bathroom is too small or tight, try to figure out ways to create more space. This is not always possible, but maybe going from a sink cabinet to a pedestal sink will give you more space to move about. Or maybe the elongated toilet bowl is too big for the bathroom and you need to switch to a round toilet bowl giving you more floor space in front of the shower. Another thing to consider is maybe you don't need a bathtub in the hallway bathroom. Perhaps you can convert to a stand up shower and gain cabinet space for linens?

As you can see, function is a big reason to remodel a bathroom. Think about how you can make the bathroom more useful and not just prettier.

Style

A stylistic remodel to your bathroom with increase the value of your home if done well. If you currently have vinyl flooring, an old sink cabinet, mirror, toilet, etc., you can do wonders to your bath for a reasonable cost. Replace that flooring with a nice ceramic, stone or marble floor. The square footage is small, so if you can afford the marble or some sort of stone, it will be a big hit. Another great bath improvement to consider is tile the tub/shower surround with the same tile as you use on the floor, or one that matches. Upgrade your vanity/sink cabinet to a nice contemporary cabinet. Instead of laminate, install a stone countertop (Marble, granite, concrete, etc.). Replace the old toilet with a nice new white Kohler toilet. Change out plumbing fixtures, towel bars and hardware with nice matching pieces to compliment your new remodel. Don't forget a nice light colored paint and accent pieces to finish it off. Nice lighting is important in a bathroom too. Recessed lights are night in the ceiling combined with some sconces above the mirror and maybe another wall accenting a picture. If your bathroom is small, consider adding clear glass doors to the bathtub / shower to open up the room versus a shower curtain.

The right design and style of a bathroom can have jaw dropping results. Take your time to do this right. You can completely remodel a bathroom for less than $5000 easily including stone tile.

Add a Laundry Room on Same Level of Master Bedroom

If you do not have a laundry room on the same floor as the bedrooms, adding one can be a nice selling point. It seems like laundry rooms were put in the basement of houses for 70 years. Everyone on the 1st and 2nd floor would drop their clothing and dirty towels down the clothes shoot and wait for the clothes to be washed and carried back up two flights of stairs. In recent years, builders have been putting laundry rooms on the same floor as the majority of bedrooms. Having a laundry room on the same floor as the bedrooms makes so much more sense. If you can work it out with the plumbing (water supply lines and drainage) and power for the washer and dryer, your new laundry room will turn heads. Washing clothes will no longer force family members two flights of stairs down into the basement or a dingy laundry room to wash clothes.

Dormer the Master Bedroom

Adding square footage to your master bedroom can have dramatic results and increase the value of your home. If your main bedroom is on the top floor of your home with a decent amount of crawlspace next to it, you might have an untapped treasure waiting to be unearthed. The crawlspace next to your main bedroom could be used to enlarge your master bedroom to add more needed space or possibly a walk in closet or bath. Whatever your home needs, this is a great opportunity to expand your square footage without the pains and expense of an entire addition. Some crawl spaces are 5 feet wide with a slanted roof over them. Imagine this 5 foot wide space that spans the 15 foot length of the room opened up. That is 75 square feet added to your bedroom if you create a dormer over that crawl space. You can add windows, a large his and hers walk in closet, a sitting room, etc. The possibilities are endless. The extra square feet could create a dramatic difference to an average master bedroom. In fact, a dormer in a bedroom will create a master bedroom from a standard sized bedroom that was once looked at as a space bedroom.

Paint Master Bedroom

A fairly simple and inexpensive way to spruce up a home is to simply re-paint the most important bedroom in the house, the master bedroom.

Painting is a great way to improve your master bedroom because it can be done in one to two days and does not require outside assistance unless you have higher than normal ceilings or extensive millwork that may create some complexities when painting.

The key to repainting your master bedroom is to make it a nice bright and neutral tone. Create a neutral atmosphere that will appeal to the largest audience.

Add Master Bath to Bedroom

A master bath is an amenity that will give your home an edge over most others. A bathroom off the master bedroom is a luxury that many homes do not have.

There are multiple ways to gain a bathroom off of the master bedroom as shown below:

Connect to an existing bathroom

Do you have a bathroom next to your main bedroom that shares a wall? If so, converting this bathroom to a master bathroom might be the least expensive method to creating a bath off the master. All you need to do is create a door or passageway from the bedroom into the bathroom. If you do this, you can leave the existing bathroom entry door, or for more privacy, you can remove the door that allows public access and seal it up with drywall and paint. As long as you are not forced to place the new door in an awkward place going into the bathroom, the results can improve the value of your home for a reasonable cost.

Chop up an oversized master bedroom to add a bathroom

If your master bedroom is large and you think you can spare some space, you could consider adding a wall (basic framing), door and some plumbing to create your master bath. If you need to save space, plan your build out carefully to include a nice vanity, toilet and standup shower with a glass door if possible. Your master bathroom does not need to include a bathtub or dual vanity to be considered a master bath. If you can tile the floor and shower walls, it will look even better than drywall or vinyl. Creating a bath from extra space in a bedroom will cost more money than opening a wall to create a door to an existing bathroom, but is still less expensive than our next couple ideas.

Convert extra space adjacent to the master bedroom into a master bath.

Some homes have rooms adjacent or attached to their main bedrooms that are non-useful spaces due to their awkward size and shape. Or maybe you have an extra large walk in closet that you can chop up to convert into a bathroom? Lastly, you may have a large bedroom adjacent to your master bedroom that would not be effected too much if you borrowed some of its space for a master bath. Whatever the case, this extra unutilized space can be used to create a master bath off the main bedroom and add value to your home. In many cases, you can fit an entire full bath into these spaces with proper design.

Create a dormer to make use of crawl space

If you have attic or crawl space adjacent to your bedroom walls, you might be able to dormer your bedroom to add enough square feet adjacent to your bedroom allowing you to create a bathroom. The downside is that you will need architectural drawings, permits, a roofer, new siding, exterior paint, interior paint, plus all of the other elements that are part of the bathroom addition. This method creates a considerable amount of value, but at a cost. Do some research in your area (possibly with the help of a real estate agent) to determine whether the addition of a master bath will earn you enough value to offset the cost of this large undertaking.

An Addition to the home

Very similar to adding a dormer to create a master bath, some people will actually create an extension of their home to create an additional bathroom. I almost didn't mention this because of the extreme cost of this method. It would hardly be worth the cost unless your home was short on bathrooms or if you are able to not only create a gorgeous master bath, but maybe also an attached walk in closet or spa like bathroom giving your home a big advantage over competing homes. You will have the same expenses in this method as you will in creating a dormer, in addition to the costs of foundation work and more.

Add Built-Ins / Organizers to Bedroom Closets

A nice improvement to you home for a reasonable cost is closet organization systems or built-ins. Closet organization and built-ins include features like shelving, drawers, hangers and slots for different types of clothing items. A closet well appointed with a nice organization system is very impressive and will lure buyers that have pride in their clothing and an organized closet space.

There are two ways to get closet organization systems installed in your home:

Do-it-yourself

If you are handy, there are many places to purchase closet systems that you put together and install yourself. From home improvement stores and hardware stores to storage and furniture stores. You can find closet storage systems as a whole or you can customize yourself by purchasing different sized shelves, hanging rods and drawers to create the perfect closet to fit your space. As with any of the ideas in this book, be sure that if you take on one of these projects yourself that it must look solid and professional, or it will actually have a reverse effect on the intended appeal.

Hire a company to install

If you are not up to the challenge of installing your own closet organization system then the solution is simple. On your computer, do a search for closet organization and you will immediately find multiple companies eager to earn your business. These closet organization companies will come out, take measurements and develop a customized closet plan for each closet you wish to upgrade and quote you a price for the equipment and install.

Weigh and measure the cost of doing it yourself versus hiring a company to install custom organization to determine whether this is an improvement worth making. Closet organization will definitely appeal to home buyers, but if it costs you too much money and raises your basis, then you might decide it is not worth the trouble and expense.

Create a Master Bedroom

Early I mentioned remodeling a master bedroom as a whole and in part. However, some homes may not even have a master bedroom. You might be able to create a master bedroom.

The master bedroom is a bedroom that belongs to the head(s) of the household. In some cases it may feel like a retreat. Some master bedrooms have large walk in closets and/or bathrooms attached. They are typically the largest bedrooms in the house and contain features such as vaulted ceilings and sitting areas for getting away from louder parts of the house or for rocking a baby to sleep.

If you do not have a designated master bedroom, choose a bedroom that seems to have the most potential and reinvent it. What can you do to make it more of a master bedroom? Can you make it larger? Vault the ceilings. Install a flat screen television in the wall? Replace the carpeting? Attach it to a bathroom or walk in closet? If you can take a bedroom and set it apart from the rest with amenities and attractive finishes, you will increase the value of your home quite a bit. The cost of this project can vary from $500 to $15,000. Depending upon if you just need to replace carpet and give a fresh coat of paint to revise a room that has the potential to actually taking down walls to add master baths, walk in closets or sitting areas, it is hard to guesstimate the expense of this improvement until you have an idea of what you wish to accomplish.

Complete Master Bedroom Remodel

The master bedroom is typically the largest bedroom in the home and will often include amenities that other bedrooms in the home don't share. The spaces, such as a walk in closet or bathroom, are only accessible from the master bedroom. Because of their larger size, a master bedroom will be large enough to include a large bed, full furnishing and possibly a sitting or changing area.

The primary purpose of the master bedroom (an oversized bedroom with various amenities) is to create a getaway for the heads of the household. Everyone enjoys privacy from time to time and a master better has typically been a place to getaway after work or early in the evening before bed to relax.

A recently remodeled and well appointed master bedroom will be attractive to: buyers who have kids and require a space to get away from the noise or parents who want a bathroom that the children don't use. Your potential buyers might be a couple that has dreamt about having a large walk in closet to store their precious clothing or a buyer that has a large bedroom set in search of the perfect master bedroom to set it up in.

Buyers will be looking for a light open space with as many amenities as possible. In this book I break down the different things you can do in a master bedroom to increase its potential. Some of these items are new flooring, the addition of a bathroom, vaulted ceilings, a dormer to add square footage for a bathroom, walk-in closet or additional sitting space. Spend money in this room to make it perfect and if needed, hire the assistance of a designer to help pull it together with flawless design and neutral color choices.

Master bedroom remodeling can include basic changes from wall and floor coverings to structural changes that will completely convert the functional use of the space. Your master bedroom remodel may be completed with the simplest of changes to flooring and paint. Any improvement to your master bedroom is an overall improvement to the house. As you can see, you can easily spend upwards of $20,000 to remodel a master bedroom, or do the basics for $1000-$1500 which also improves the space on a budget.

Add Railings to Stairwells

Safety features such as railings are always a good idea to have in a home. Whether you are selling your home or planning to live in it for the long haul, you don't ever want to fall down the stairs or have a guest fall down the stairs. Not all of your buyers will be young spry people that run up and down stairs with ease. We have to keep in mind that most home buyers are older folks that will notice safety features like railings on the stairwell to avoid future spills down the steps.

Pre-cut railings can be purchased at the local hardware or lumber store. The same stores typically sell the hardware that goes along with the railings. The railings at the store come in eight foot lengths. To install them yourself, all you need is a saw to cut them to the perfect length and a screw gun to attach the hardware to the railing and then the railing to the wall going up the stairwell. You can add a basic railing to your stairwell for less than $200. You can leave the wood raw or for a more custom look, I recommend that you paint the railing a nice glossy coat of paint to match your trim (typically white or off-white). The railing will look much better with a shiny coat of paint on it and feels better as you grab onto it for support.

Smoke Detectors

Working smoke detectors will not necessarily improve the value of your home, but it is illegal not to have working smoke detectors in the appropriate places of your home and smart to have.

Be sure all of your smoke detectors are placed according to the laws of your city planning department. All smoke detectors should be operating and have fresh batteries. Even if your smoke detectors are hardwired to your electrical service panel, they still require fresh batteries to function properly and not chirp intermittently while people are viewing your home for sale.

Smoke detectors are required in every bedroom and on floors without bedrooms. Smoke alarms should be installed in or near living areas, such as family rooms and living rooms. Most people have the false impression that smoke detectors should be installed in the kitchen. This is not the case unless you want to hear the smoke detector go off every other time you cook. Smoke detectors are meant to alert you in other areas of the house away from the kitchen when there is an emergency. If you are in the kitchen, you already know there is a fire and probably don't need a smoke detector to tell you.

Install Security System

Add a security system to your home to improve its value. The optimal type of security system is a hardwired security system which can detect if windows or doors are opened or broken. The least expensive type of security system is the wireless type (installation does not require fishing wire through walls) which also work well, but the large battery powered sensors are in plain sight and not very attractive. Hardwired systems are more expensive systems for the reason that you cannot see them and they are possibly more reliable. If a home is already built and access is limited, most people with opt for the wireless security system so they do not have to put holes in the walls to run wires.

A basic security system that notifies the home owner of a break-in is great and can cost less than $1,000.00. However, the improvement to your home will be limited versus the installation of surveillance. Surveillance cameras for home security are becoming more popular in average homes as more companies are getting into the business. The prices have come way down and you have the ability to watch your cameras from cell phones and computers anytime you want. A home surveillance system can be purchased at electronic stores or online if you want to install yourself. Or you can hire a professional to install the surveillance system and help get it all set up on your phone and computer. Just like the basic home security system, surveillance cameras and equipment can be wireless or wired. It is better to have your cameras hardwired if possible, but again, this will mean putting holes in walls and running cable throughout certain spaces of your home to achieve this.

My personal recommendation is that if you want to add a security feature to your home to improve the value of your home, go all the way and install the home security combined with surveillance. It can be done for less than $2,000. However, if you want to get cameras that are full color and clear streaming with no pixilation, including a digital recorder that records up to 3 weeks of video information, you could be looking upwards of $3500 or more.

Plumbing: Repair or Completely Update

In order to get top dollar for your home, the big ticket items have to be updated within a reasonable time frame so your buyers will have comfort in knowing they will not have any large expenses looming around the corner. One of these large ticket items is plumbing. If your home has old galvanized plumbing and you are seeking top dollar for your home, I recommend re-piping the entire house. A home inspector will always warn a buyer of the gloom and doom of galvanized pipes. Buyers will second guess the purchase or your home or could ask for some sort of discount or rebate to cover their cost of updates.

There are a few ways to tell if you need to re-pipe your home aside from basing this decision solely on the age of your plumbing: your water pressure is low, your water is discolored, rust particles can be seen, your pipes are visibly corroded or they are leaking. Some old galvanized pipes are so close to failure that when you go to repair them, the surrounding pipes begin to leak at the joints due to corrosion.

Old pipes are a liability on your home. Aside from fire, water is the next most destructive threat to any home. Old pipes can leak inside the walls causing serious damage to your home. This damage is multiplied if it happens when you are away from the home for a long period of time. The damage to your walls, floors, ceilings and personal items can be in the tens of thousands of dollars.

If you come to the conclusion that you need to re-pipe your home, you have several material options:

Copper pipe

A new copper pipe system will not rust or corrode like the older galvanized iron pipe. Most plumbers are familiar with and trained in the installation of copper pipe. Copper pipe is easy to install and access to it is common at most home improvement stores. Re-piping with copper isn't just economical, but it can improve your health as opposed to galvanized pipes. As iron pipes rust, this leads to rust flaking off and contaminating the water as it travels through the pipes. You will not have this problem with copper pipes as they should last for the remaining life of your home if installed well.

Pex

Pex is a polyethylene piping system that is becoming increasingly popular in homes today. Not all plumbers have the tools or know-how to install it, but it is worth seeking out the plumbers that do because Pex is a fantastic product and less expensive than copper.

PEX is clear plastic-like tubing which is made from cross linked high density polyethylene polymer. PEX has several advantages over metal pipe (copper, iron, lead). It is flexible, resistant to scale and chlorine, doesn't corrode or develop pinholes, is faster to install than metal and requires fewer connections and fittings. Installation of PEX plumbing does not require heat to bond the pipes. A ring is crimped over the piping using a hand tool instead of a blowtorch. If you are going to re-pipe your home, you should definitely consider re-piping with Pex.

Electrical: Repair or Completely Update

If your wiring is old and out of date it can be a fire hazard. Old wiring will be a red flag for buyers seeking a turn-key home. If your wiring is outdated and you know it will be an issue, you may want to consider rewiring the entire house. Rewiring a house does not always mean you will be replacing your electric service panel, but there is a good chance you will because the panel is probably the same age as your old wiring.

An example of old wiring that should probably be replaced by now is knob and tube wiring. Fairly common in houses built before 1930, the knob and tube system uses porcelain insulators (knobs) for running wires through unobstructed spaces. Porcelain tubes protect wires that run through studs and joists. Knob and tube wiring was a great system for its time. However, because of how old it us, it tends to get modified and spliced over the years changing it from its original layout. These changes to knob and tube wiring make the wiring unsafe because the changes are typically done without taking into consideration the exact load each wire should have, etc. When additional branches or fixtures are added, the fuses protecting the old circuits are likely to blow frequently. Installing larger fuses is commonly done, but unsafe, solution. Oversized fuses allow much more current to flow than originally intended, resulting in additional heat in the conductors. This heat causes the insulation protecting the wire to become brittle, and eventually to disintegrate. Both of these issues create fire hazards.

Other later types of wiring can be faulty or disorganized and in need of replacement. Perhaps a house was built after knob and tube was popular and it had the current wiring of its time. Or maybe knob and tube was replaced in the 1950's or 1960's. The wiring can still be faulty and in need of repair. Just like with knob and tube, when wiring in the house gets spliced into, added too or re-routed enough times as the house changes and owners change, the wiring and electrical system becomes compromised and unsafe. There comes a time in every house where the wiring is in need of a complete overhaul.

Rewiring a house could cost from $7500-$15000 depending upon the size of your house and access to all the different floors. Rewiring a house is a lot easier if you have a basement with exposed ceilings. If your basement ceilings are finish, then this will be an even more difficult task. You will have to weigh your options and maybe consider selling your house at a discount versus spending all of your money to replace the wiring. It will cost you the same either way.

Upgrade Electrical Panel (Breaker Box)

The electrical service panel is a crucial point of any home. The quality of the service panel determines both the safety of your home and the smooth operation of your electrical system.

The electrical panel, also known as the breaker box or breaker panel is a metal box that houses a number of circuit breakers that distribute power throughout your home. Circuit breakers control the power to your home by turning on and off to protect wires from damage by "tripping" when an electrical short or over usages of outlets in your home occurs.

If your circuit breakers are old or dated, the wiring is exposed or appears out of sorts, or if you feel like you don't have enough power to certain rooms of your home, you may consider replacing your electrical panel or adding a sub-panel. If your electrical panel is out of date or not safe, it will be noted in an inspection report and you may be asked to replace it anyhow.

The cost of a box and breakers from your local hardware store ranges from $100 - $200. The replacement of an electrical panel has to be done by a licensed electrician. While the cost of the materials is not that high, your ultimate cost will be determined by the electrician that does the job and what his/her labor costs are. Be sure to get a couple of bids before you choose an electrician. The entire cost (labor plus materials and permits) varies between $500-$1500 depending upon the complexity and size of your job.

Obtain Planning Permission on Prior Improvements

If you made improvements to your home that increased the number of bedrooms, bathrooms, square feet or any other large improvement requiring permission from the city, you should be able to provide permits to prospective buyers in case they request it. If you make an improvement and your city or state does not know about the improvements, then your home will still be viewed and valued the same as it was before the improvements you made by the city and state. Online websites that value your home use data from the city and state to determine the worth of your home because it used public data to obtain square feet, bedrooms and bathroom in your home. If you do not obtain permits, then this information is not updated to public websites. When prospective buyers look up your house online to get an estimated value of your home, the websites will give a number lower than your home is actually worth.

Another issue is that obtaining a permit for work done on your home tells a buyer that you improved the home according to code. Improving a home according to code means the home was inspected by the city and the owner did not have the option to cut corners. This pertains to additions, large improvements, plumbing improvements, electrical improvements, dormers and more.

Many people skip the city planning permits because permits cost a bit more money and it raises property taxes once the city realizes your home is worth more. However, if buyers know that you made big improvements to your home, not all, but some buyers will demand to see permits and if you cannot provide them, they will pass on your home or attempt to negotiate a lower price.

Level House Out

Do your floors lean one direction or another? If you set a marble on the floor, does the marble roll to a corner of the room? If so, you may have settling and foundation problems. Depending upon where your home is located, you could face issues with the ground settling if the ground beneath your home is moist. Over the years, your home will experience sloping floors and unlevel floors as the posts beneath your home slowly sink and settle at different speeds. Sloping floors are temporarily curable. The cost of the cure/solution will depend heavily on access to the space beneath the house. If the space beneath your home is easily accessible with the posts and beams exposed, it may not cost much money to level out the house again. However, if access is limited beneath your home (it should be if your foundation is post and pillar) it may cost you a lot more money to level out your home. Understand that if your floors are sloped or your home is leaning, buyers will be expecting fixer property pricing. No matter how nice your home is, buyers will be very weary of a home that leans. Even if it costs $10,000 to level out your floors, it is something you should highly consider if the sloping is noticeable.

Another reason your floors may be unlevel or slope could be due to insect damage or wood destroying organisms such as dry rot. The fix in this situation will be similar to the above fix of gaining access beneath the house and jacking up the house in the spots where it is low. However, in this case, you will not just be able to fix the house by jacking it up. An additional step will be required to solve the problem. You will need to replace any wood that has insect damage, infestation or dry rot. Once this wood has been replaced, you must treat the crawlspace to prevent the damage from happening again. Unfortunately for me, I have had experience with both of these situations. I spent less than $3,000 both times. The cost of the entire project will depend heavily on where you live and who you hire. Large construction companies will charge and arm and a leg, while you may be able to find an individual that is licensed and bonded that can do this for you at a fraction of the cost of a big construction company.

Clean Windows

Clean windows will make a world of difference. Many of us get used to looking through dirty windows. It doesn't take long for the rain, pollen and dust to dirty our window exteriors. On the same hand, the inside of our windows get very dirty as well with hand prints, head prints (from peering out the window at our neighbors), foggy from stale inside air and foggy from oil or gas heat furnaces. Regardless of the reason, cleaning the windows inside and out should most definitely be on the list before you market your house for sale. You will be amazed at the difference a good window cleaning will make. The windows virtually disappear before your eyes. When you are cleaning up the windows, you have two options with the window screens (if you have window screens). The first option is to have your window cleaner (or yourself) remove, spray, wipe down and reinstall the screens. Screens get incredibly dirty over time and will catch all of the dirt and dust that blows through the air on a daily basis. Another thing that I like to do with the screens when selling a house is to take them all off and store them. I prefer the look of a house with shiny clean windows and no screens. Take off all of the window screens, label them with some blue painters tape and store them all in the house somewhere out of site. Your house will photograph better and will have better curb appeal without screens blocking your nice clean windows.

Repair Holes and Cracks in Plaster and Drywall throughout Your Home

Cracks are very common in plaster walls. Drywall usually does not bear cracks unless your house has experienced extreme settling. While drywall does not typically crack, it does easily dent and scratch if bumped into. The fix for both is the same and very easy.

Plaster repair

For long cracks in plaster I recommend paintable caulk over spackle. The cracks are inevitably going to get bigger and you want a product that is going to stretch with the crack so the crack does not show again for a long time. For cracks larger than a quarter inch wide, you will have to use some sort of spackle or plaster filler to fill the gap. Once the cracks are filled nice and tight, sand any excess filler above the surface, prime and paint.

Drywall repair

Drywall repair is very easy and the supplies are readily available at most hardware stores because it is so common in today's homes. If you are patching a hole, kits are available for purchase with screens to cover the hole. You affix the screen, and then apply a couple thin layers of drywall mud (which you can buy in different size pre-mixed pails) to the area. Once you have applied a couple good smooth coats of mud over the area and it is completely dry, use a sanding sponge to sand down the area as smooth as you can. Prime and paint the patch to match the existing wall. If you can see the patch after simply painting the patch because the paint is not exactly the same as the color currently on the wall, you should repaint the entire wall for uniformity.

If you only have cracks or dents in your drywall, you can probably get away with one pass over of spackle using a putty knife. Sand, prime and paint the area to complete.

If your wall is textured (whether plaster or drywall), you can buy a can of spray texture and texture the wall before you prime to match the existing texture. The can of spray texture has a nozzle on the tip to adjust the size of the texture. You should test out the texture by spraying it onto a large piece of cardboard until you create a perfect match by adjusting the nozzle back and forth. Then follow the instructions on the can of texture and spray the wall. Allow the texture to dry completely before priming the wall or the texture will wipe away with your paint brush or roller.

Remove Texture Coated Ceilings

Textured ceilings are common in older homes. Since a ceiling makes up one-sixth of a room's total area, a textured ceiling can be an eye sore since most textured ceilings are highly unattractive and old. Updating your home's ceiling will increase a room's appearance greatly while improving value at a low cost to you. I am talking about popcorn ceilings which are the textured ceilings with shiny specs in it. It is typically dirty, dusty and full of cobwebs because if you try sweeping it, you will get dry chunks of texture in your eyes (not fun). Sometimes the material that has been blown onto the ceiling can contain toxins like asbestos. Regardless of what it is, textured ceilings are not in any more and must go.

If you are removing the popcorn/textured ceiling yourself, and want to be sure it is not toxic, you should chip a piece of the texture off of the ceiling and have it tested for asbestos. Regardless of whether the texture has asbestos in it, you do not want to inhale any of the product into your lungs, so it is best to treat it as if it was toxic anyhow. There are two ways to get rid of the texture: The hard way and the easy way

The hard way:

To begin, you need to remove everything from the room. Tarp off the floor with a large plastic tarp and tape the side of tarp about 1 foot up the wall on all 4 sides of the room. Then use painter's plastic to tarp off all of the walls of the room where the bottom of the plastic overlaps the floor plastic. Then you will need a pump sprayer, floor scraper, painter's overalls and a respirator. Once you've got your painter overalls on (protective painter clothing you get for $20 at a home improvement store that goes over your clothing), fill the pump sprayer with water. Pump the sprayer up and start spraying water onto the ceiling. This turns the texture/popcorn ceiling to a muddy substance. Now take the floor scraper and carefully scrape along the ceiling to remove the texture. It should come off easily. You may need to repeat this process in order to get all of the texture product off the ceiling. Once you have removed all of the ceiling texture, take off the painter overalls and throw onto the floor, remove all of the plastic from the walls and place in the center of the floor tarp. Now roll up the floor tarp into a large burrito type package and dispose of properly. If you discover that your ceiling had asbestos in the texture, you must research the rules for proper disposal of the hazardous waste product.

The easy way:

I found out the hard way that this was possible and kicked myself for not thinking of it first. What I am about to tell you is a very easy and clean way to get rid of the textured ceiling without the toxic mess. Many people will simply install a layer of 1/4 inch or 1/2 inch drywall over the texture ceiling and hide it with a new ceiling (a new layer of drywall). This is genius not only because it takes a fraction of the time and reduces the mess, but many times the ceiling has been textured to hide large cracks which have formed over time. A new layer a drywall will not only hide the texture, but it will reinforce the integrity of your ceiling as well.

Replace or Install Window Coverings

Window coverings can make a room look large, bright and open, but also small, dark and outdated. Many people overlook window coverings not realizing the impact they have on room. Bedrooms should at least have some sort of mini-blinds or curtains for privacy. Some basic light curtains can make a bedroom look cozy. The main living spaces may or may not look good with blinds, but should have some sort of light or neutral toned curtains to create privacy when it is needed. Replacing or installing window coverings can get expensive depending on the quality of the materials required. Some people may choose an inexpensive route of simple white or cream aluminum blinds on all of the windows for privacy (stay away from cheap plastic mini-blinds which discolor quickly). If you have a high-end home or want to add some design to a room, you may end up spending a few hundred dollars per window installing higher quality blinds or curtains.

Curtains can cost more than blinds because you need more materials to complete and they are time consuming to install. Curtain rods can vary in price, but if you want them to look good, you are going to pay $50-$150 per window. Your curtain panels will cost $50-$150 each as well depending upon where you shop for them. If you do not have a history of making good design decisions, get the opinion of someone that does when picking out curtains (colors, textures & style). I don't pretend to be a good designer. That is evident when I try making design decisions on my own. If you do not have access to someone with interior design assistance, nor can afford to pay someone, then thumb through some home interior magazine and you will be surprised at how much you will learn and absorb.

Coved Ceilings or Crown Molding

Architectural elements on the ceiling can have a dramatic affect on any room. There are a couple of architecture additions you can add to your ceilings to accent a room: Coved ceilings or crown molding. Coved ceilings and or crown molding will give any ceiling a more sophisticated look and feel.

Coved ceilings

A coved ceiling is an architectural detail where the top of the wall rounds seamlessly into the ceiling. The drywall or plaster bends into a 90 degree angle to meet the ceiling. Cove ceilings are more common in old homes and create a classic and elegant look for your home. Coved ceilings must be framed underneath your joists and trusses. Coves can be installed in dining rooms, master bedrooms and living rooms. Coved ceilings can be combined with crown molding for an even richer look.

Crown molding

Crown molding is basically trim for the ceiling. It comes in a multitude of thicknesses, shapes and styles and is installed around the border of the ceiling to create an elegant transition from your walls to your ceiling. Crown molding can be compared to picture frames in that they frame the ceiling and are available in many different styles. Crown molding is fairly simple to install as long as the ceiling and walls are square. If you are installing crown molding in an older home, it gets more difficult because you may not be working with straight lines and surfaces. Regardless, crown molding can still be installed in older homes, cheaper than coved ceilings, and can be a cost effective way to quickly upgrade an average looking living room, dining room, bedroom or more.

Archways & Architectural Improvements

Architectural improvements such as archways are admired features of a home by a high percentage of buyers. When reading property listings and descriptions, you will notice that the real estate agent always mentions the beautiful archways a home has. Archways are mentioned in the limited description because they are an important feature of a home that shows a home has desirable style elements. Most common in older homes, archways are seen in multiple shapes and styles.

Most common archways are half rounded. Some archways are rounded more at the edges and straighter in the center, or rounded sites and come to a point at the top or may simply consist of two diagonal horizontal lines that meet at a higher point in the center. The different style archways are done for a reason by the builder at the time and may be a reflection of the style of home or cultural influence of the builder/remodcler of the home.

If your home was built without an archway, but you think your home could benefit from one (or more), they can easily be installed by a contractor or handyman. Archways can be constructed using basic framing and drywall. In some cases, archways can be built completely out of millwork so you don't have the mess of framing, drywall mud, sanding and painting.

Below I describe some (but not all) different styles of archways found in homes:

Half-round archways

Half-round archways are a perfect half circle, as the name implies. This style of archway is often associated as bringing a Spanish feel to a home.

Elliptical archways

Elliptical archways have distinct features from the half round archway. The elliptical archway has a gentle curve in the center and sharper curves in the corners. This style of archway is often associated with bringing an elegant and lavish feel to a home.

Eyebrow or segmented archways

Eyebrow archways look like a section of a larger circle. This archway has often been associated with bringing a modern and contemporary feel to a home.

In addition to the archways mentioned above, some archways consist of unique features such as columns or pillars on either side creating a more dramatic entrance to a room.

Install or Replace Baseboard Trim

Brand new fresh base trim can make a world of difference in a home. In many cases, homes are absent of any base trim. Sometimes baseboards are made of thin cheap plastic or wood products that are outdated, worn down, or have so many coats of paint on them, you can't tell where the wall stops and the trim starts.

MDF if an inexpensive trim product that is easy to cut and install and relatively inexpensive to buy. There are many wood and MDF options in the baseboard department. Some people like short 2-6 inch tall trim, while others may prefer an 8 or 10 inch tall trim (common in older homes).

Installing baseboard trim can be done relatively easily without the help of a professional. However, you need the right tools to cut and install trim and to remove old trim if needed. The tools you need for the job are a tape measure, chop saw and pin nailer. If you are familiar with these tools, you can install the base trim yourself for the low cost of the supplies and your time. Otherwise, I advise hiring a handyman or carpenter to assist. If you want to do it yourself, I have listed the steps below:

If you currently have baseboards (cheap or in bad condition) remove the old baseboards in the room using a flat pry bar and hammer. Slide the pry bar between the wall and baseboard and tap the pry bar until you have a little gap worked open. Continue tapping the pry bar down until you cannot go any further and begin to pry the trim off the wall. If you feel your pry bar about to crack or break the drywall or plaster while removing the base trim, try putting a flat object behind the pry bar such as a piece of metal or wood to prevent damage to the wall. This will give your pry bar leverage without it crushing your wall. Repeat down the length of the base trim as needed.

If you have decided to also replace or install trim around the doors, continue removing all of that trim the same way as mentioned above. Be very careful and do not dent or put holes in the walls with your hammer or pry bar.

Measure for all of the trim you will need. Purchase the trim and bring it back at your home. One thing that most professionals when installing base trim is to layout all of the trim and pre-paint it. Because base trim is installed just above nice hardwood or carpeted floors, painting it in advance will prevent you from having to paint all of the base after it is installed and risk getting paint on the floor. If you paint the trim in advance, then after the trim is installed, you only have to touch up the seams and nail holes.

To begin installing your trim, you will start with your longest base lengths. Measure your longest length, cut your piece and nail into place. If you have basic base molding with no extra details, your job will be very simple. You will just keep measuring cutting and installing the base trim along the walls and around doors. However, if your trim has detailed edges on it, you will need to cut the corners of your trim at a 45 degree angle so that the trim matches as it turns the corners in your home. Getting your cuts down perfectly will take some time and patience. It seems easy to make the simple adjustment on your chop saw, but getting your corner seams to line up perfectly will have you pulling your hair out. Especially if your walls are not perfectly square.

Once you have completed install all of your base trim, it is time to make it look even better. Because most houses are not perfectly square, you can have gaps at your seams even if you make perfect cuts on your saw. If you are painting your base trim, I suggest filling all nail holes, seams and gaps with paintable interior caulk to hide all seams, including along the top of the trim. Be sure your caulk is very smooth. You want the caulk to look like it is part of the wood when you touch up paint over it. You can also use filler, spackle or wood putty over the nail holes for a smoother look. Once the caulk or filler has dried you can touch up those areas with paint. Trim is usually painted with Semi or hi-gloss paint because it takes a beating and you want it to be easily cleanable.

The end result will be gorgeous. If you never had base trim prior, you will be amazed at the results. Even if you are replacing old inexpensive trim that the builder or preview home owner installed, the finished product can be a stunning change compared to what you were used to.

Install or Replace Window Trim

Just like base trim, window trim is a highly important feature in every room. Painted, stained or raw wood surrounding a window enhances the beauty of your window and your room in its entirety. If you don't already have trim around the interior of your windows, you should highly consider installing it or having it installed by a professional. The cost is fairly inexpensive for the return on investment. Just like base trim, installation can be very simple to do as long as you have basic carpentry skills, a tape measure, chop saw and nail gun.

Below I will explain a two different ways to trim out your windows:

The most basic windowsill plate:

If your windows are currently trimmed or trimmed simply with drywall around all sides, you can add a windowsill or apron at the bottom. You may be able to install the wood trim right above the bottom piece of drywall. However, this may block the bottom of your window frame and look strange. If this is the case, go ahead and remove the bottom dry wall piece and replace it with your trim piece. You can use finish grade lumber or MDF (primed fiber board) to make your windowsill plate. Once cut and installed into place, paint the windowsill with a strong semi or hi-gloss paint to protect it. Many times people will utilize the window sill to decorate or set plants on, so you want a durable paint that can easily be wiped clean.

The windowsill plate is typically cut to a width one inch wider than the distance from the face of the window to the face of the wall, and one inch longer than the distance between the two side pieces of the surround. In other words, you want it to hang over an inch or so towards you like a small shelf and an inch past the left and right side of the window. You will need to cut notches in the wood to get the windowsill plate to have the appearance that it is wider than the window.

Complete window trim surrounding all four sides:

Decide on the style of trim that you would like to wrap your windows with. You can get the basic flat pieces of wood trim (primed or unprimed) or decorative trim, which will be more difficult to cut and install perfectly. After deciding how you want to trim out your windows, start taking measurements and cutting all of your pieces. All of the windows should be trimmed exactly the same. Take advantage of book stores and libraries to look through books and magazines fill with photos of homes and window trim to gain inspiration and ideas. You will find the most basic trim with four flat sides up to the most extreme trim with multiple layers of decorative wood. I suggest you keep it simple since you are merely trying to spruce up your home to sell for the least amount of time and money out of pocket. Choose a small detail and get to work making each and every room in your house look dramatically better with some new window trim. Once your trim is installed, fill all cracks, gaps and nail holes with putty or caulk, then paint with a semi gloss or hi gloss paint.

Add Interior Trim & Millwork

If you home is absent of interior trim or millwork, you can greatly improve the appearance of your home by installing interior trim and millwork. One of the most noticeable features of any home is the interior trim. Installing nice trim and millwork can add an air of elegance and sophistication to any room, door or window.

There are three main types of trim installed in a home: Window & door trim, crown molding & Base molding. All three types of trim can greatly improve the look, feel and value of your home.

Window & door trim:

Window and door trim is the trim that frames your windows and doors creating a nice border around them. Interior trim is available in a variety of styles and materials (metal to wood). The majority of installed pieces are made from wood and each type can add dimension to a room, depending on the type installed, and where it is installed. When trimming out windows and doors, there are multiple methods by which you can choose from. The architectural style of your home should determine the trim style you choose. If you need ideas there are loads of pictures in design books & magazines and online that can help you determine what combination of trim will look the best around your windows or doors. There are also different complexities that will determine whether you decide to install the trim yourself or hire a professional. The complexities will be the type of corners you choose to have. If you are using decorative trim and you want the line around the windows or doors to be continuous, the cuts of your trim will be more customized and it may require the assistance of a carpenter. Trim can be installed successfully with just straight cuts too. Do your research and decide for yourself which trim style works best and then determine if this is a project you want to take on yourself or hire out.

Crown molding

Crown molding is the molding that borders the ceiling of your rooms. It is a popular choice when you want the ceiling of a room to appear higher than it actually is. Crown molding is installed where the wall meets the ceiling; it gives the illusion of the wall ending at the base of the molding, while the ceiling rises on above. It is often coupled with dentil molding, a decorative trim that adds detail to the illusion and often hides shadows created by the crown molding.

Base Molding

Base molding is trim installed at the base of the wall, to cover gaps between the wall and the flooring and to provide a finished appearance while framing the floor. It is usually used in conjunction with shoe molding; a type of decorative trim meant to conceal an uneven floor (typically called quarter round).

Good architectural molding installed inside the home can reflect the quality of the craftsmen who built the home and/or the decorating style and taste of the owners who installed it. From sweeping decorative trim framing the ceiling of a room to well chosen window and door trim, nothing can beat its elegant simplicity in creating a showcase out of a simple home. If the interior of your home does not have any trim, or the trim is cheap and flimsy, you should definitely consider a trim makeover to win over buyers.

Install Updated Light Switch and Outlet Covers throughout Your Home

Electrical light switch and outlet covers serve as both an important safety feature in the home, while also completing the finishing touches to each room. They help protect the user from getting electrocuted by the dangerous electrical wires that make up the switch and outlets. They reduce the risk of accident or harm to persons or animals in the home. Replacing old light switch and outlet covers is a simple and inexpensive way to freshen up the look of your home. Over time, outlet covers show their age and start to become dirty, discolored, cracked and broken. Replacing your outlet covers can provide a positive contribution to your home at a very affordable price.

Outlet covers are available at most hardware and home improvement stores. When purchasing new light switch and outlet covers you will notice many different colors and styles. As with paint, flooring and other materials that go into your home, the wise choice is to go with white or cream colored switch plate covers. The best option is if you can match the outlet covers to the trim/millwork. White or cream will always be your fall back color since most light switches and outlets are white or cream.

Replacing light switch and outlet covers is extremely easy. You just need a flat head screw driver and the new outlet covers. You unscrew the current outlet covers and screw on the new ones.

Brand new shiny outlet covers will provide you with a final touch showing that you have a well cared for home. Outlet covers are a small improvement, but for the price you can't afford not to do this.

Install Updated Light Switches and/or Dimmers

Most homes have the single pull light switches and circular plugs. To update your home and give it a more contemporary look and feel, considering upgrading to the rectangular large light switches and outlets. Give your light switches and plugs a fresh makeover with these larger switches. Plugs & plate covers are available that match. The popular name for these rectangular switches and plugs is Decora.

If you have an older home with original push button or turn dial light switches, you may be able to find new replica replacements at a local home store such as Rejuvenation Hardware.

Dimmer switches can be a great improvement, but do not really have an impact on the value of a home. Dimmer switches are great for dining rooms, bathrooms and living rooms to control ambient light. The cost of a dimmer light switch can vary from $20-$40 as opposed to $1.50 - $4 for normal light switches.

Repaint Entire Interior

When trying to sell your home, repainting your interior should be at the top of the list because of its impact on your home and potentially low cost. Real estate agents and interior designers strongly recommend painting a home in neutral colors to help it sell faster. Neutral colors are light and clean colors such as white, cream, gray, clay, beige, tan, etc. Neutral colors make a home look open, clean and inviting. In addition to the positive first impression neutral tones create as a buyer steps into your home for the first time, they also make a property look best in photographs online and in print; the places where potential buyers see your home for the first time and make the decision to take the next step and look at your house or condo in person. Lastly, many home buyers want a turn-key home and do not want to have to repaint the interior after closing and before moving in your home. If your walls are coated in colors they do not like (dark colors, vibrant colors, primary colors, etc.), then the potential buyers will start adding up the expenses of repainting your home when weighing their options to buyer your home.

Paint Important Rooms - Neutral Tones

If painting your entire home interior is out of your budget or out of the question, you should at least consider a fresh coat of paint on the important rooms such as the kitchen, living room, etc. If you watch any home shows whatsoever, they always instruct you to remove the personal colors and re-paint all walls to neutral tones. The reason is that you are trying to appeal to as many people as possible. The most common and acceptable colors are white, cream, tan, taupe, beige, etc. Neutral tones appeals to the largest audience. You want the largest audience to like your home. In addition to creating rooms with the most generic colors possible to appeal to the masses, the colors mentioned also make a room brighter and more open as opposed to colors like, green, blue, red and so on. You and 15% of the buying population may love the red living room or the green kitchen, but 70%+ buyers like light neutral tones on their walls. That is the sector you want to appeal too.

Painting rooms neutral tones is such a great way to improve the sales value of your home because it has a great impact at a very low cost. While you may need to hire a professional to repaint your entire interior, you may not necessarily need to hire a professional to paint a couple rooms. All you need is paint and painting supplies. A common color combination is white or cream trim (base trim and window trim) with off-white or tan walls. For great color combination ideas, visit your local paint store. Some paint manufacturers have color guides for neutral tones because they are so popular right now.

Upgrade Lighting

Lighting is an extremely important part of the home's interior in many ways. Lighting shows whether a home is outdated or recently remodeled, efficient or non-efficient, bright or depressing, cared for or forgotten. The cost of this improvement will vary depending upon the depths you want to delve into your lighting and just how outdated your lighting is. One of my biggest turn offs is fluorescent lighting in a dropdown kitchen ceiling. Even worse is when the kitchen is in the middle of a house and the only source of light is the buzzing fluorescent ceiling panels that make someone feel like they are sitting in a middle school.

Brightness

We will start with the simplest lighting solution which is brightness. Your rooms should be well lit with lights. If you don't have enough light, consider adding more lighting. Install lights that allow high wattage bulbs or take least 2 light bulbs. Some ceiling light fixtures only take one bulb. Your goal is to create more light, so one bulb will not suffice, therefore, when looking at ceiling light fixtures, be sure to purchase the fixtures that take a couple of 60 watt bulbs. Two bulbs will not be an efficient use of energy, but our goal in this section is to brighten up your living spaces. If home efficiency is a concern, you can use fluorescent light bulbs.

Update lighting

Another lighting improvement is the exchanging of outdated lighting to newer types of lighting. The most common upgrade in lighting starts with ceiling lighting. Many people prefer to replace old ceiling lights with recessed lighting. Recessed lighting immediately modernizes a room. Recessed lighting (also known as can lights) comes in a variety of shapes and sizes. Recessed lights can be directional to highlight a painting on the wall, or point straight down to flood a room with light. Wall sconces are also great to light up hallways and stairwells. Sconces also add character to living rooms, dining rooms, surrounding fireplaces, surrounding beds in a bedroom and more. Once you begin looking at different styles of lighting you will be amazed at all of the options available. And remember, if you are looking for lighting with the intention of selling your home; keep your style choices clean and simple. To keep costs down, you can replace many different light fixtures yourself if you are familiar with basic electrical. Recessed lighting will take more work and require an electrician to hardwire them in and connect to the light switch. Installing recessed lights into an existing ceiling can be a little messy with drywall or plaster dust in addition to the insulation that will drop out of the ceiling and wood shavings from drilling. However, when all of the work is done, it is worth it.

Efficiency

Another lighting improvement is the improvement of the efficiency of your lights throughout your home. Both your lights and light bulbs can be upgraded or adjusted to be more efficient.

For years, fluorescent bulbs gave off a cold sterile light and were inexpensive. However, due to the increasing price of electricity and awareness of the environment there is a higher demand for efficient lights and bulbs. Efficient lights and bulbs have evolved and become a much nicer product. Efficient bulbs are more expensive than standard bulbs, but they give off warm light now versus the cold sterile light that most of us are used too. New eco-friendly homes have special lights and bulbs installed in them. Whether increasing the efficiency of your home will improve the value of your home is based solely on your buyer. Some people will not care about efficiency as much as they will about style, whereas your more eco-conscious buyer will love it.

Flooring: Replace Old Floor Coverings with New / Updated Flooring

Replacing the flooring in your home is a great way to make a big improvement quickly. There are lots of different products available whether you are seeking a new hard or soft surface for your home.

Carpeting

Carpeting over 5-7 yrs old should probably be replaced; especially in some of the main rooms, stairs, etc. It should be easy to tell if your carpet needs replacing. If you cleaned the carpet and you can still see the high traffic areas, then it is time for a replacement. If you have pets, get an honest opinion from friends whether your house has a pet odor. If so, this is another indication that you should definitely replace your carpets. If you decide that you need or want to replace your carpet, then replace your carpet with light neutral tones; the lighter the better. Carpet can be installed rather inexpensively unless you choose an expensive brand.

Vinyl flooring

Vinyl floors (also called linoleum floors) are available in a huge variety of colors and styles. Vinyl flooring is excellent in bathrooms and kitchens. This type of flooring has an ease of installation and is the most affordable of all flooring. As an alternative to flooring with ceramic tiles, vinyl floors give the same look as tiles, except they cost less than ceramic tile. I would not recommend going from tile to vinyl, but if you already have vinyl that is in bad shape, then consider choosing a more contemporary high quality vinyl to replace what you currently have in place.

Laminate flooring

Laminate floors are floors that look like hardwood floors, but are actually a manmade substance that can be more resistance to damage, sound proof and easy to install. Laminate floors are the fastest growing choice of flooring in today. Laminate flooring became popular in Europe and now it is increasingly popular in the United States. Laminate floors are cheaper than hardwood and they are easy to maintain. Laminate flooring is virtually resistant to burns, scratches, chipping and is great for high traffic areas.

Tile flooring

Floor tiles come in ceramic, stone and marble. Tile flooring is great because it is durable, waterproof and can be easily cleaned. I prefer tile flooring in entrance ways, kitchens and bathrooms because of its durability and ease to clean. You will have fun choosing from all of the different styles and colors. When done well, flooring tiles are a dramatic improvement to a home and in a kitchen or bath, 10 times better than vinyl flooring.

Hardwood flooring

If you have the budget, solid hardwood floors are the most popular and most desirable floors. Because of the natural beauty and durability of solid hardwood floors, they have been used to floor homes for centuries. Solid wood floors are a timeless investment that can produce a lifetime of beauty and add value to any home. Wood floors come in Maple, Pecan, Beech, Cherry, Oak, Pine, Birch, Walnut, Hickory and many more unique woods from around the world.

Bamboo flooring

Bamboo is an eco-friendly choice versus hardwood floors. Bamboo is not wood, it is actually considered grass. Bamboo is very durable, elegant and versatile. The natural variations of color that is unique to bamboo come from carbonization and are usually a honey brown color or light tan. Bamboo flooring is not very expensive and does not require refinishing. It comes pre-finished so you don't have the sanding and chemicals involved in refinishing hardwoods to your liking. The downside is durability. While bamboo can last a long time, it will easily dent and scratch if you have a rock or something hard stuck to the bottom of your shoe.

Cork flooring

Cork is a naturally harvested product that comes from trees in Portugal and Spain. Cork is retrieved only from mature trees. Cork is considered a renewable and sustainable natural resource. It can be colored in any shade because it absorbs stains easily.

Interior Design with a Professional

We all like to think that we are experts at designing our interior spaces. However, when it comes time to sell your home while trying to get top dollar for it, it can be a wise decision to spend an hour or two with a professional designer to be sure your home is staged to perfection. A professional designer can give you tips on the paint colors, window coverings, de-cluttering your space, lighting options and more. Keep an open mind and allow someone with an unbiased eye help you make your house more marketable and desirable.

Increase the Visual Square Feet of Your Home

It may not be so easy to physically increase the square footage of your home, but you may be able to give your home the appearance of having more square feet over a weekend. The size of your home dramatically affects the value, but square footage isn't the only space that counts. Visual space or how large a home feels is equally important. You know right away what I am talking about because you have been in a two bedroom condo that was only 650 square feet and thought it was over 1,000 square feet; because of it layout and tidiness. The same holds true in reverse. A poor layout or design can make a large space feel small. The key is to make each room in your house feel larger.

There are a few ways to accomplish more visible space:

- Add a mirror to the room to give dimension
- Replace heavy draperies with blinds
- Clear clutter. Get rid of items that you don't need in the room.
- Floor coverings should have plane or no patterns on them. More patterns make a room feel small.

Regardless of what you do, make your space feel open and vast and most people will perceive your rooms as larger than actual.

Bring the Outdoors In

A majority of home buyers want to feel like their indoors are a part of the outdoors. It just makes you feel happier to be in a home where lots of natural light is able to flow through the home. The main way to accomplish this is through the use of your windows. A large view of the outdoors will make a room feel larger. Be sure blinds and curtains are not obstructing window views. Keep clutter away from windows so you can see larger views. Consider turning two standard windows into an opening for French or sliding glass doors. Lastly, a lot of trees or foliage outside your windows can block out a lot of your much needed light. Have your trees trimmed or thinned out (professionals cut branches even throughout an entire tree plus any branches or foliage touching house) around your windows to allow more light to flood your rooms.

Vaulted Ceilings / Exposed Beams

Vaulted ceilings and exposed beams are sought out features in a home. Do you notice how people mention vaulted ceilings and exposed beams any opportunity they get in a real estate listing or property description? This is because vaulted ceilings give a dramatic feel to a room. Vaulted ceilings with exposed beams can make a room feel palatial as opposed to rooms where the ceiling is just above your head.

You may not have the option to create vaulted ceilings or exposed beams unless you have a pitched roof above a room in the house. Whether it be a living space such as a kitchen, living room, dining room or bedroom, a vaulted ceiling is a moderately priced improvement.

Most of the work can be done without much experience to save money. If you decide to take this on yourself, you will begin by demoing out the ceiling of the room you wish to add an exposed ceiling or vault. The key is to not remove anything that appears to be giving support to the roof. This means that you can remove the ceiling drywall or plaster on your own and dispose of it. You can also remove the insulation to expose the bottom side of the roof and its supports. At this point you would want an experienced professional to take over and create the structure for your vaulted ceiling. If you want an exposed beam or skylight, this can be arranged at this point. Once the framing is done for the vaulted ceiling, you will have the insulation and electrical for any lights reinstalled. Then drywall and paint. The entire process should not take long if you are only doing one room.

Make It Brighter

While elements of this topic have been mentioned in other parts of this book (lighting), the topic is important enough to stand on its own as a way to increase value or your home and command a higher sales price for your home. A bright home will always be more appealing to buyers versus a dark and dreary home. How can you make your home brighter? Below are a few ways to do it:

- Increase the wattage of your light bulbs.
- Add more lights fixtures and lamps throughout the home.
- Paint rooms with light paint colors to make rooms brighter and appear larger.
- De-clutter your home around lights and windows
- Keep curtains and blinds open to allow as much light as possible to come in.

By doing all of the above, your home will brighten up and become a step closer to appealing to more buyers.

Make Sure Every Light Bulb in the House Works

Be sure all of your light bulbs are functioning and bright for two reasons: Bright rooms create positive perceptions and burnt out light bulbs can look trashy and paint the picture of an un-kept home.

In this book I mention brightening up your home by opening blinds and curtains, more lighting, lighter paint colors, etc. However, if you want to brighten up your home for the least amount of money, make sure that every light bulb in your house is the highest wattage your light fixture can take. Each light fixture has a sticky label right on the light socket that says: Max 60 Watts or Max 100 Watts, etc. If your light fixtures take higher wattage light bulbs, go ahead and upgrade to create brighter rooms for a small investment of $20 - $60.

Replace burned out bulbs. Be sure all the bulbs in your ceiling lights, sconces, refrigerator, oven hood, etc. all work. Small things such as burnt out bulbs may tell potential buyers that this is not a well maintained home. If you aren't replacing bad light bulbs, then what other sorts of maintenance issues have you been ignoring?

Another factor to consider with bulbs is to always use warm light and not cold light. Even with fluorescent bulbs today, you can get bright warm colors versus the old bluish light that they used to emit. Be sure all bulbs are warm colored.

Lastly, be sure to pay special attention to all dark areas such as basements, attics and crawl spaces are well lit so potential buyers can see all of the hidden potential in your home.

Deferred Maintenance

It is time to fix and repair all of the things in your home that are in need of attention. Many of these items may be things that you have learned to cope with over time, but may turn off potential buyers. You may be so used to some of the quirks in your house that you will need a non-bias opinion from an outsider to determine what is working properly and what needs to be repaired before putting the house on the market. It might be a good time to replace that hole in the bedroom door, fix the door that won't shut all the way, fix the window that won't open all the way, tighten the knobs falling off the cabinets, etc.

Check the outside of the home. Is your fence standing up straight and working property? Do you need to replace any steps on the front porch? Are your house numbers tightly secured to the house?

Buyers want to buy a house that is turn-key. Unless you are selling a fixer property at a discounted price, be sure there is nothing in need of repair the day your home goes onto the market. As mentioned before, items in need of repair will be highlighted in the inspection report anyhow, so you might as well take care of them now.

Deep Clean Your House

A thoroughly clean home should be at the top of your list of home improvements because of its importance and low cost. A clean house shows that the home owners maintain the home well. Buyers will be more able to imagine themselves in your home if it is spotless.

The best part of all, a deep clean will barely cost you anything but your time. A thoroughly clean home with increase the buyer's perception of your home. The best option to ensure that your home is deeply cleaned is to hire a professional cleaning company. A professional cleaner may go beyond what a typical home owner considers to be clean. If your time is limited, the cost will not be that bad ranging $200 - $400 depending upon the size of your home.

A deep clean is more than a wipe down of a home. It will require detailed cleaning in every room of the house to include items such as faucets, countertops, microwaves, blinds, backsplash, window sills, the oven, under the fridge, baseboards, laundry room, etc. Below I have provided a list of different areas of focus for each room of your home:

Baths

- All tile should be cleaned
- Clean tile grout with mildew cleaner.
- If the tub caulk is darkened, replace it.
- If white tub finish is dark, clean with bleach
- Replace shower curtains
- Clean shower doors to remove any and all residue
- Clean plumbing fixtures
- Clean toilet
- Clean mirror
- Clean floor
- Wipe down walls

Kitchen

- Clean all appliances. If appliances are stainless, use a special polish and do not use an abrasive or your appliances will scratch.
- Replace stove burner pans
- Clean the inside and outside of the oven
- Wipe down cabinets (inside and out)
- Defrost (if necessary) and clean the refrigerator
- Clean the microwave (inside and out)
- Clean hood or range vent
- Clean flooring and countertops

Floors

- Floors throughout the home must shine
- Worn hardwoods should be refinished or cleaned and clear coated. Do not use wax or any floor cleaners on wood floors. They are all bogus and leave a cloudy film on your floor. Just use warm water mixed with ammonia.
- Deep clean your carpets. If they do not look good afterwards, replace them.

Walls

- Clean walls the best you can. Use the cleaning sponge to wipe off scuffs and dirt. If that doesn't work, you may need to repaint some walls to make your home sparkle again.

Storage Spaces & Garage

- Remove all debris
- Get rid of all clutter
- Sweep or shop-vac to clean floors and cobwebs

Remove or Control Odors

Hopefully you don't have odors in your house. If you do have odors in your home, try to find the source and solve the issue. Unfortunately, some houses embody odors and if yours is one of them, you will want to get rid of it before you allow potential buyers to preview your home.

To remove odors, you can start by doing a deep clean. A deep clean is required before selling a house anyhow. If a deep clean does not remove all odors from your house, you may consider an air purifier. Open the windows and create air flow. Clean the furnace filter and let the furnace circulate the air through its own filtration system. An air purifier is a device which removes contaminants from the air. Air purifiers employ a variety of technologies to remove impurities from the air. The most common air purifiers employ a simple filter to clean the air. The filter can be pulled out of the unit, cleaned and replaced. While this type of filter may not be effective for cleaning the air, it may not be effective in removing odors from the air. The best type of filter for removing odor is an ionic filter or electrostatic air cleaner. An electrostatic air cleaner uses an electrically charged panel or screen to capture particulates. Another type of air purifier, called an ionizer or ion-generating air cleaner, attaches an electrically-charged ion particle to dust and other pollutants, making the particles heavier and causing them to drop from the air. These machines really do remove odors from your home. The only problem is that these machines have an odor of their own. The air will have an electronic odor as a result of using either of the electronic air purifiers. Because of the electronic odor in the air from the ionizer, it will be obvious to potential buyers that you are trying to hide an odor of the home.

Some people may choose the good old fashioned method such as plug in air fresheners, air freshener sprays and potpourri. Air fresheners do not solve a problem, but they will temporarily mask it. If you are in a time crunch and cannot figure out what the odor is in your house, or maybe you don't even have an odor, but you want to spruce up the experience viewing your home, utilize an air freshener to bump up the vibe of your home.

Install or Replace Your Doorbell

A doorbell is an important feature in large homes. A properly functioning door bell will notify everyone in the home of a guest no matter how far they are from the door. Guests don't like banging on a door to notify you they are standing outside waiting for you. Make your house more functional by adding or replacing your doorbell.

Add a doorbell

If your home does not have a doorbell, two types of doorbells can be installed. One option, which is the more expensive route, is to have the door bell hardwired in. Hardwiring a doorbell means that the doorbell will be connected to your electrical system with the wiring routed through the walls, floors or ceilings of your home. The wires will be hidden and you will never have to replace batteries. However, if access or money is an issue, there is another option. The less expensive option is to purchase a battery powered door bell that requires no wiring. The doorbell button gets screwed to the exterior of your front door wall and the doorbell gets attached to a wall on the inside of the home. The button and doorbell both take batteries and work wirelessly. Wireless doorbells work very well, but may not be as elegant as an expensive hardwired door bell.

Fix or replace the doorbell

Another option is to fix a door bell that currently does not work well or upgrade to one that is a lot nicer. Upgrade your old door bell to one that better fits the architecture or style or your home. Perhaps you can find a door bell that has a better chime to it. Regardless of the reasons, be sure that your existing door bell works and is an attractive one with a good audible tone.

Refinish Hardwood Floors in lieu of Replacement

A cost effective way to brighten up the home and increase the value is the refinishing of hardwood floors. The cost to hire a company to refinish your wood floors can be surprisingly low in most cases. You can bring the cost down even more by renting a floor sander from a local equipment / tool rental facility and do it yourself. I have both hired contractors to refinish floors and have rented machines to do it myself. If you are on a tight budget, go ahead and do this yourself, but you have to be very careful when using the floor sanders yourself for the first time. A lot of things can go wrong and your floor could end up with gouges and dips in it from the drum sander sanding too deep. Sanding your own floors with heavy machines takes finesse and practice to avoid causing damage to the wood. You also have to remove the base shoe or quarter round when using the edger (sander) to sand along the walls and corners. The edge sander is very heavy and will destroy your lower back within a couple of hours. Sanding down the floors can be done within one day. However, you could go through a lot of sandpaper in the process. Once you get all of your materials and rent your equipment, you may be able to refinish your floors yourself for a cost of approximately $500 versus spending $1100-$1400 to have a professional company refinish them for you perfectly. The difference in cost is nearly double, but in the grand scheme of things, $1400 will be a small price to pay to increase the value and positive perception of your home as people walk through and the sun and lighting is reflecting off of your brand new looking floors.

Create or Add a Sunroom

A sunroom is room that allows you to experience the beauty of the outdoors while enjoying the benefits of the indoors. The sunroom provides a greater amount of natural light than any other room in the house with a variety of large windows, sliding glass or French doors and skylights. The natural light and views of the outdoors can be enjoyed year around from the indoors where you can control the climate. Many people use these rooms to grow plants, as an additional TV room, dining room, children's playroom, workout room and more.

Sunrooms are becoming more and more popular additions to homes. A sunroom can be created at a low cost by making slight changes and renovations to your home or by form of an addition for considerably more money.

If you are on a budget and want to create a sunroom in your home, you will need to start by scouting out a location in your home that will work. For example, many people will take a front or back open air porch and close it in with windows and a door. The windows may have the ability to open for airflow in the summer and close to keep in the heat in the winter. If you are creating the sunroom from a porch, be sure to upgrade your flooring and be sure all seals are tight to keep out the unwanted climate and insects.

In addition to the closed in front or back porch sunroom, some homes may have a back room that can be modified by adding windows, glass doors or skylights to create a sunroom. While both of these options are the least expensive way to add a sunroom, they will still cost a sizeable sum of money to ensure that the sunroom will look like it is part of the house. To do this you need to be careful and decisive in your modifications using well thought out and cohesive finishes.

If space is not readily available within your home, you may consider setting aside a budge to add on a sunroom to your home utilizing special framing. Special framing materials are available for creating sunroom add-ons to homes. The most cost effective sunroom add-on can be done using aluminum framing. Aluminum is a common metal used to make sunrooms. You may have seen this type of sunroom over and around swimming pools in warm states such as Florida and Arizona. For more money, you can add a complete addition out of wood framing, double pane windows and a foundation. Unfortunately, this will cost almost as much as a complete addition to your home, so the return on your money may not be that great unless you feel under certain circumstances that your house will not be complete without a sunroom.

Create a Dormer

Unlock the hidden potential in your home to expand a room, bathroom, bedroom or office. Wasted space is common in older one and a half story homes with high pitched roofs. Lately it seems as though homes are built with more space and complete second floors as opposed to older homes where the 2nd floor is riddled with slanted ceilings.

A dormer can be a costly undertaking since a dormer has to be constructed by licensed contractors and follow land and development codes specific to where you live.

First you must determine which type of a dormer is going to net you the largest increase in value of your home. For example, maybe you have a home with 3 bedrooms on the top floor and no bathroom. It would make the most sense in this situation to create a dormer in one of the bedrooms to create additional square feet to add a bath. Or maybe you only have two bedrooms on the top floor, but it would make sense to have three bedrooms to appeal to the family with two children. Again, by creating a dormer in one of the bedrooms, you can expand one of the bedrooms into two bedrooms if there is enough room. Creating the perfect house for the next potential family is essential to getting the most money for your home.

Last note on adding a dormer is that you will need an architect to help determine if you can in fact add a dormer and to help create the dimensions for your builder. In order for your to add the additional weight of a new room expansion, an architect or engineer will have to check the walls and support structure beneath the proposed expansion to be sure you are able to add the additional weight without compromising the integrity of the home.

Adding a dormer is an expensive improvement, but the result could net a higher return than your investment if your plan is well thought out by creating a much needed functional space.

Add an Extension to Your Home

Adding an extension to your home can significantly improve the value of your home as long as it is well built and cohesive with the existing home and property.

The unfortunate situation is that an extension will cost a considerable amount of money because you are actually extending the footprint of the home which means that you will have to order a professional set of plans, obtain planning permits, pour a foundation, frame the new structure, insulate it, side it, roof it, install windows & doors, etc.

While adding an extension to your home will have a tremendous effect on the value of your home, it will require a considerable investment. The return on investment is almost guaranteed to exceed the expense as long as you are adding much needed square footage to add rooms or make rooms larger, etc. An extension can cost upwards of $30,000 to $100,000 depending upon the size, complexity and materials used.

Remove Walls to Expand Space

Does your old home fall victim to too many walls? Do you have too many small closed off rooms and not enough large open spaces. If so, you should consider the thought of removing a wall (or walls) to open up a room. The most common wall removal option which results in the biggest benefit to value is typically opening up the kitchen to an adjacent living space. Kitchens in many older homes are closed in by four walls. There is usually a swinging door or small pass through in between the kitchen and the dining room. If you can remove that wall and door, the improvement could be dramatic. The new large open space would make both rooms more enjoyable to be in. People that enjoy cooking do not want to feel like they are hidden in a back room somewhere while preparing a meal for family and/or friends.

The same wall removal/expansion can be done to combine two small bedrooms into one large dream bedroom. You could open up a wall between a sitting room and a small office or den that you barely use. More and more people in today's market are demanding large open spaces as opposed to many small rooms.

Removing a wall is not that costly. However, unless you are very familiar with framing and electrical, it may not be a project you will want to take on alone. The wall you choose to remove may be a load bearing wall. A load bearing wall is a wall exists to bear the load of the weight above it. If a wall is a load bearing wall, it does not mean that it cannot be removed. It just means that you will have to install a header. A header is a horizontal beam (thick lumber) placed over a window, door or opening (like in this case) which supports the weight above the opening in lieu of a fully framed wall. It is recommended to have a professional remove a load bearing wall and install the header to your opening. Once the header is in, you wrap drywall around the opening or finish with trim creating a more elegant and sophisticated look. Finish with primer and touch up paint for an opening that appears as though it has always been there. I cannot begin to tell you how much of an improvement removing walls can make in many homes. When flipping older homes, removing walls is one of the first things investors seek out to immediately improve a home and modernize it to today's standards.

Wall Coverings: Update or Remove and Paint

Wall coverings are making a resurgence. More and more people and interior design professionals are using wall coverings / wall paper to spruce up a room. It seems as though a number of decades have past where remodelers and home owners revolted against wall paper and coverings. Wall paper was torn down, scraped off the walls and the walls were painted with custom colors, sponges and accent walls.

Today, people are using wall paper to add style, texture and dimension to a room. While wall paper used to be inexpensive and printed in boring common patterns, today's wall paper reaches new levels of sophistication with rich grass cloths, hand-painted papers and murals. High end designers and scrutinizing home owners are using these types of wall coverings to add warmth, dimension and sophistication to their homes. You can borrow ideas from home and design magazines. There is no shortage of images in design magazines that show great uses of wall coverings.

Carefully chosen and installed wall coverings will show your home in a positive light and hopefully inspire buyers to pinpoint your home over all others on the market.

Repair Old Windows

If you are selling an older home with original wood windows, be sure the windows function properly. Over time, wood windows get painted shut, the weights that hold the windows open do not function any more, window tracks fail, etc.

Windows stuck shut

If a window is painted shut, there are several ways to get the window to open and close again. One way is to use a utility knife to cut around the board of the window frame where it is painted shut. They can work pretty well, but you have to be very careful not to slip with the knife and mark up the window frames with the knife. The issues I have had with a knife are that while you are cutting the window loose, a knife does not particularly remove the paint or obstruction. The knife cuts the window loose, but it is still typically so tight that the window does not slide well.

Another great way I discovered to cut windows loose is by using a Fien tool. It is an amazing small handheld tool that you plug into an outlet. It comes with a multitude of different tips to use on it depending upon the project. The tips are blades that saw with a rapid back and forth (left and right) motion. The tool has blades that not only cut right through the paint holding the window shut, but it sends the debris flying out of the space so after you use it on an entire window frame border, your window is loose and will slide up and down freely as it should. Not only does the Fien tool work, it makes the job go by very quickly. You can do an entire house before lunch time. The downside to this tool is that it will definitely leave some marks. You may need to do some touch up paint afterwards. Just don't paint the windows shut again.

Window weights don't work

Other issues with wood windows are that the weights inside the wall may have become disconnected so the window does not stay up on its own. For the sake of selling the house, it might not be important reattach the weights in the windows, but if you want to rectify the situation so your home is fully function, here is what you can do. To re-attach the weights to your window ropes you need to pull off the interior trim around the window to gain access to the ropes and weights to reattach them. Once you have the front trim off, you should be able to see the rope and the weight in the wall. If the old rope is still good and the weight is available, tie the weight back on and be sure it functions properly before carefully nailing the trim back on around the window. If the rope or weight is missing or in disrepair, window ropes and weights are available at hardware stores for purchase.

Window off Track

A third issue with wood and vinyl windows are the tracks and springs. Sometimes windows fall off their track and need to be fixed by the manufacturer. If you bought the windows yourself, you should have a warranty for situations like these. However, if you did not buy the windows yourself, then the warranty on these windows will be void and you will have to track down the manufacturer and pay to get them fixed or replace them. When tracks go back in vinyl windows, they will not open up straight or even stay open for that matter.

Making sure all of your windows operate effectively is a wise decision to show you are a good caretaker of your home. In addition to showing people that you care about details, people will be pleased that they can easily get airflow or a cross breeze in the home if they want too. Buyers will be deterred by a house with inoperable windows.

Change out Window Hardware

Do you have old window hardware on your windows that barely works or has been painted over so many times you cannot even tell what kind of metal it is made out of? Home improvement stores, hardware stores and even home furnishing stores sell window hardware. In most cases all you need to replace are the window handles and window locks. Window hardware comes in a multitude of different colors, metals and styles. The easiest thing to do is to determine the style of your home and purchase the hardware to match. The most popular hardware styles are chrome, brushed nickel, brass and oil rubbed bronze. Those are just a few of your color and metal choices. Beyond that you have a variety of styles that begin with the simplest of styles to the absurd (deer heads, branches and ladybugs). Stick with the most basic hardware to appeal to the largest audience. As long as all of your window hardware is simple and new, it will make the good impression you are seeking to improve the value of your home.

Replace Door Knobs, Hinges and Cabinet Pulls throughout and where Needed

New door knobs, cabinet hinges and handles can tighten up the polished look and feel of your home as you prepare to sell.

Door Knobs

Many of us don't realize the various styles of door knobs in our homes. Or maybe you have gotten used to the old door knobs that don't work well or have become tarnished, scratched and chipped over years of use. Regardless of the situation, a home should have presentable and functional door knobs; Presentable door knobs for aesthetic reasons and functioning door knobs for safety and privacy.

The pricing of door knobs will vary from $20 to $150 per door knob. A couple of things that will effect door knob price are the door knob style and its function. Door knob styles will vary from the most basic round handled brushed satin chrome finish and brass knobs to the more elegant styles and finishes such as oil rubbed bronze, glass, etc. handles. Door handles also vary in function which will affect the price. For example, bedroom and hall closets will require a door knob that does not lock. Bathroom and bedroom doors will have locking mechanisms and cost 20-30% more each.

When making the decision to replace door handles, you will need to set a budget and then determine if you can afford to replace all the door knobs to look the same and consistent throughout your home. If you do not have many doors and you can replace them all under budget, then you should consider increasing the quality and style of your door knobs throughout the house to impress your potential buyers.

Hinges and cabinet pulls

If you have built in cabinets anywhere in your home, then you should take a look at the hinges and handles to see if they should be replaced. In older homes, the hinges may have been painted over so many times you cannot tell the difference between the millwork and the hinges. The same goes for the handles and knobs on old built in cabinetry. It is common for the hardware to have been painted over. If your cabinet hinges and knobs are in bad shape, you have a couple of options: refinish the hardware or replace it.

Refinish the hardware

The first and least expensive option is to salvage the hardware. In older homes, it is not uncommon to find that the old hinges and hardware are quite nice and just need to be cleaned. If your hardware is nice, but has multiple layers of paint over it, you might be able to remove the hardware and put them in paint stripper and remove the paint. You could end up with nicer hardware then anything you would buy from a store at a reasonable cost because yours is original and goes with the style of the house. Sometimes the hardware will be too far gone, worn and damaged. However, in most cases, people think the hardware is too far gone, but after the layers of paint slide off with one coat of paint stripper, they learn that the hardware is beautiful and makes the built in cabinetry relevant again.

Replace the hardware

The second option is to remove the old hardware and replace it all with new hardware. Cabinet hinges, handles and knobs are sold at home improvement stores (big and small) and hardware stores. Some stores will only sell generic replacement hardware. However, there are stores such as Rejuvenation Hardware that specialize in selling cabinetry hardware that replicates hardware from the different decades to match the era and style of your home with new hardware.

If you are going for a polished look inside your home to please the picky buyer, new door knobs and hardware are a great way to go. I recommend you price out the hardware and door knobs before you start removing them from your house. While hinges and door knobs are not expensive on their own, the cost will add up quickly once you start trying to replace all the hardware in your home at once. Then you must decide whether the improvement is worth the expense.

Weather-stripping

In this book I have an entire section on insulating your house. However, if you are on a budget and want to make an inexpensive improvement that will save a significant amount of money on utility bills, then weather-stripping is the way to go. Can you feel the breeze coming in through your front or back door? Can you see light coming in through the border of your door along the bottom sides or top? If you answered yes to either of these questions, you need to apply weather-stripping to your door. There are a few different types of weather-stripping you can use on your door.

Sticky foam tape is the weather stripping that comes in different thicknesses. You can apply it along the sides and top of the door to create a snug fit when closed. This will solve the issue of both light and air passing through the border seams of a door. Another good weather-stripping for the sides or top of a door are metal strips that nail or screwed to the side or top of the door frame. These metal strips have a rubber piece that presses against the door when the door is shut preventing air from escaping. Both of these options are great inexpensive options to weather-strip the top and sides of your doors.

If you can see light or feel a breeze through the bottom of your doors, you need to purchase and install a threshold at the bottom or attach a door sweep to the bottom of the door. Both options are easy, but if doing this yourself, the door sweep is the easiest because it can simply be cut to length and screwed to the door. A threshold is a little more difficult to both install and make look professional. A threshold comes in metal or wood and will often take more than a few cuts to make it fit perfectly within the door frame. Thresholds have a padded rubber center to them that pushed up snug against the bottom of the door protecting you from the elements outside.

Insulate the Home

If you own an older home, then there is a high probability that your exterior walls are not insulated. If this is the case, you may want to consider having the walls insulated. Whether you are trying to retain heat in the winter or cool air conditioning in the summer, good insulation is the solution to trapping these luxuries in your home. Heat and air will escape through walls, windows and doors if not properly insulated.

Make your home more energy efficient so that the desired climate you are paying for on the inside of your home does not seep out the doors, walls and windows and become costly to maintain.

There are a number of ways to insulate your home:

Weather stripping

Weather stripping is a type of insulation that is applied around door jams and windows that open and shut. One type of weather stripping for doors and windows is a foam type that comes in different thickness and widths. Other types are weather stripping are rubber or a combination of metal and rubber such as thresholds that go beneath the door when you shut it.

Double pane windows

Double pane windows as opposed to single pane windows are considered a type of insulation. The compressed air that is between the two windows acts as insulation. When the seal is broken, the insulation value is diminished and the windows will have a foggy appearance.

Most common insulation is the insulation in your walls, floors and ceilings. There are major types of insulation for walls, floors and ceilings: Blown in or loose fill insulation, rigid board or blankets and bats. The type of insulation material that you use will be dependent upon many factors, such as where in the house you are using it (Ceiling, floors or walls) and code requirements.

Blown in or loose fill insulation

Loose fill insulation is a type of insulation that is either blown into the walls or ceiling, or poured in and spread. This type of insulation looks like ground up newspapers and is made up of fiber and pellet mix. The product can be made of natural material such as recycled cotton or wool. One of the main benefits of loose fill insulation is that it can be blown into tight areas that are hard to access. Tight areas could be crawl spaces, ceilings, attics, walls that are already covered. On older homes that do not have insulation in the walls, this is a popular method to fill the walls with insulation. The professional will drill holes along the walls along the exterior or interior of the house in between each stud and using machine and a hose, they can blow the insulation into the walls completely filling them up. The downside to this type of insulation is when you have to put holes in the walls or ceilings to do any remodeling, the insulation pours out of the walls and snows out of the ceiling making a huge mess. It is a great product if you never have to see it again after you use it.

Blankets and batts

The most common insulation is blankets and bats insulation. It is the pink or white insulation that looks like cotton candy. This insulation is made of fiber glass and is pre-cut to fit perfectly in between floor joists, wall studs and ceiling rafters. You can purchase this type of insulation in rolls or strips. This type of insulation is not very expensive and very easy to use as long as the space you are trying to insulate is fully exposed (new construction or remodel). The insulation can be purchased from local home improvement stores and comes in multiple pre-determined widths to fit perfectly in between your studs or joists. Blankets and bats are easy to cut and use. The big downside is that the insulation can get into your eyes and skin if you don't wear protective clothing and goggles. Any part of your skin that is exposed will feel itchy afterwards. You have to rinse will cold water to get the fibers off of your skin because warm water will open up your pours and allow the fibers to dig in even deeper. The sensation can be compared to getting a haircut and having small hairs under your shirt all day long before you get a chance to shower.

Rigid board or Styrofoam insulation

Styrofoam insulation is an insulation type that is common in ceilings. It is thinner than blanket or bat insulation (maybe 2 inches thick) and has the same insulating value as a thick piece of blanket or bat insulation. It works well in roof top rafters or dormer roofs because your roof needs to breath. Notice your roof has vents (it should have vents). These vents allow air to pass through the roof / attic area. Attic ventilation is an important part of roofing. Proper attic ventilation extends the life of a roof and reduces problems because it minimizes the temperature differential between the attic and the air outside. Proper ventilation will remove moisture and heat from the attic. In addition to the venting you already have in your ceiling or attic space, Styrofoam insulation can be applied so that there is an air gap of about 2 inches between the roof and the insulation. This allows the air to flow freely so your roof does not get too hot.

Regardless of the type of insulation you use, an insulated house will be more marketable than a non-insulated home. This is especially true in areas that have extreme hot or cold climates. While a house with or without insulation appears the same from the outside, the buyer of a home without insulation will quickly learn this news following their home inspection.

Programmable Thermostats

A terrific way to reduce heating costs in your home can be done by updating non-programmable thermostat with programmable thermostats. Often times, a non-programmable thermostat remains on the same temperature all day long and all evening long. Nobody is available to adjust the temperature gauge to your needs. If a manual thermostat is set to 70 degrees in the summer it could run while you are at work and while you are sleeping under your covers. Two times you do not need your house to be as warm as normal are during the day when nobody is home and in the middle of the night when everyone is sleeping under their covers. A lot of electricity and gas are wasted by manual thermostats that remain on unneeded temperatures throughout the day and night. A programmable thermostat can easily be programmed to increase the heat in the morning just before you get out of bed, decrease the heat around 9 or 10AM after everyone is has left the house for school and work, then increase it again around 3-4 PM to welcome everyone back home to a warm house and then turn itself back down around 11PM or Midnight after everyone is tucked into bed sleeping. The thermostat will do this every day conserving energy and saving you and future owners a considerable amount of money on utility bills.

Heat: Upgrade Heating System to more Efficient System

Upgrading your heat source to a more efficient system can improve the value of your home. A more efficient system means the utility costs will be lower for years to come. Unfortunately with products that offer more efficiency such as furnaces and automobiles (hybrids / electric), they come at a higher than normal cost. A high efficiency furnace will cost more than a less efficient furnace. The percentage increase in efficiency you get for the cost may or may not be worth it. Furnace efficiency rates range from 78% to 98%. A furnace is generally not considered high efficiency unless it is 90% or greater.

There are several reasons you may want to purchase a high efficiency furnace upgrade:

- A more efficient furnace will be attractive to a buyer because it will make the operation of a home less expensive.
- For the buyer seeking an eco-friendly home, a higher efficiency furnace makes your home a more perfect match.
- Tax rebates: gas furnaces with an efficiency rating of at least 95% may qualify for a federal or state tax credit.

The cost to replace/install a new furnace is approximately $3000-$5000 depending upon the company you go through. High Efficiency models tend to cost approximately $500-$1000 more than standard efficiency models.

If you have a perfectly good operating furnace in your home, then it may not be worth spending almost $5000 to upgrade your furnace to high efficiency. A couple reasons to upgrade your furnace would be to obtain a "green" certification on your home. Another reason to upgrade prior to sale is if your furnace is old, unattractive and showing signs of its age; upgrading to a high efficiency furnace may be a nice selling point for your home.

Heat: Change Entire Heating System from One Type to an Improved System

In many instances, you can improve the value of your home greatly by completely upgrading the type of system that heats your house from an old outdated system to a more current system which is both more efficient and space saving.

Greater Efficiency:

The former section discussed upgrading your furnace to a more efficient furnace. However, there is a much greater improvement you can make which is improving your entire heating system from one system type to another, such as oil to gas, electric to gas, forced air to radiant heat or forced air to geo thermal (I will describe the different types below).

Oil to Gas or electric heat

In many cases, if your home has oil heat, there might be a reason. It is possible that you do not have gas lines on your street and therefore oil or electric were the only options for heat. But for those of you who do have a choice, gas burns a lot cleaner and is a lot less of a hassle as compared to oil furnaces which need their tanks filled periodically for a lump sum that you may or may not have at the time. Gas is usually invoiced monthly and you don't have to check fuel levels or worry about getting to the bottom of your tank and clogging your oil lines. Homes heated by oil have a specific odor to the heat in addition to a smokey residue around the vents that the oil heat makes as it blows through the vents over the years. When you remove pictures that have been on the wall for a long time in an older oil heated house, you will often find a dark frame of oil residue on the walls. That is from the dirty oil heat air that is blowing into the house and leaving residue on the walls. In many cases, improving your system from an oil furnace to gas furnace or electric heat will make for a nice improvement to your heating system.

Forced Air Gas or Oil to Radiant Heat

Another heating improvement that may be more efficient than forced air gas or oil furnaces is gas radiant heat systems. Not only are these systems more efficient, but they do not blow air through old ductwork into home. Cleaning ductwork is not a common thing people do. This means that most homes with force air furnaces (whether oil, gas or electric) are circulating dirty air through the house every fall and winter. Radiant heat is a system that relies on convection to heat from the ground up. Radiant heat can be any type of heat in the flooring of your home or baseboards (typically installed beneath windows) that heats from the bottom of the room and radiates upwards. As the heat rises, it fills the room with a consistent heat as opposed to the heat a forced air furnace blows into your home every 10 minutes. Forced air heat blows into a room until it reaches a specific temperature, turns off, dissipates and blows in again and again. Your furnace is constantly turning on and off, blowing new hot air into the house every 10 to 15 minutes to keep you warm and maintain a certain temperature. Radiant heat seems to stick around longer in your home at a more consistent rate so you don't get warm and cold back and forth during forced air furnace cycles. Radiant heat can be electric heating elements or hot water. Electric heating elements can be installed beneath tile floors and with the use of radiators along baseboards of your home. Hot water radiant heat systems can also be installed as baseboard heat. In addition to baseboard heat, radiant hot water heat can be installed beneath your floor by running the water pipes back and forth through the floor joists beneath your floors. I installed a radiant water heat system in my house beneath hardwood floors and since I could not access the 2nd floor floors, I installed baseboard heaters on the 2nd floor. I love the clean heat that radiates off of the radiators. A couple things that I don't like is that they are not quick to heat a room when your house quickly gets cold in the evening. In addition, the heat is hard on old wood floors and will quickly dry them out and make them creaky with gaps in between the wood. Radiant hot water heat is fueled by a boiler or hot water heater in your home. A boiler is probably what you will use as it is more efficient than a hot water heater and will not have to run non-stop like a hot water heater. When a professional installs the system and sets it up for you, he or she will set the settings on the boiler or water heater at a safe temperature so your hardwood floors do not heat up too quickly and warp. My floors are not that bad after all, but I think with 100 yr old hardwood floors, I would have been better off still using radiant heat but only baseboard heaters and no piping beneath my floors.

Geothermal Heating

Another type of heat that is a recent technological advancement and can greatly reduce your energy bills over time is geothermal energy. Geothermal energy is the most efficient and cleanest way to heat your home and will be quite impressive to any potential buyers. Geothermal heat is used along with your radiant floor system or domestic hot water heating system as discussed above. The system extracts heat from the earth using a loop or series of pipes placed in the ground and connected to your furnace. The earth below the ground maintains a higher rate of temperature consistency because it absorbs over 46% of the sun's heat as it hits the surface of the earth. A geothermal heating system (furnace) is able to tap into this free energy using a system of piping installed in the ground. This type of heating is becoming increasingly more popular. The system is more efficient than other comparable heating systems because you do not have to pay for as much gas, oil or electricity to maintain the high temperature of the water to heat your home.

Space Saving

While home owners may be interested in the latest technology to enjoy cleaner homes and lower energy bills, most people also prefer a system that is invisible and takes up the least amount of space. The worst and most invasive heating systems are force air heating systems because they require large ducts to blow the warm air into various rooms and floors of your house combined with intake ducts that suck air out of your house and into the furnace to circulate the air. The combination of all these ducts means you will have low ceilings in the basement, vents in certain parts of rooms that limit furniture placement and a giant furnace somewhere in your house taking up space. Alternatives to this type of a system are the radiant hot water heating systems or electric baseboard heat. Electric baseboard heat is the simplest of the space saving heat sources because there is not main heating center. The heat is created by the baseboard heater itself and simply needs electricity and a thermostat to operate. Alternatively, some people may not want to see any heaters, because baseboard heaters still protrude from the walls and can limit furniture placement. The ultimate space saving heating system is in-floor radiant heater (whether electric or hot water). The hot water pipes are installed within the floor joists so you cannot see them whether you are below the heated floor in the basement or above them. By using in-floor radiant heat, you will create more head room in the basement opening up the possibility of a more livable basement space. The only downside to the in-floor radiant hot water system is that you still have to have the boiler or hot water heater somewhere. If you use the hot water system, you can use an on-demand heat source such as a boiler which will bolt to a wall and minimize space. The downside is that there is quite a bit of labor involved in the installation of the in-floor radiant heat system.

Whether upgrading the heating system to take advantage of recent efficient advancements in technology or to gain more needed space for furnishing your home or headspace in the basement, the cost can easily exceed $10,000 to make this improvement. You have to ask yourself and your real estate agent whether this improvement would improve the attractiveness of your home enough to offset the large cost to install.

Tankless Water Heater

A tankless (or On-Demand) hot water heater is a hot water heater that heats water when you need it without the use of a storage tank (the storage tank being the large cylindrical hot water heater tank we are all accustomed to seeing in homes). As soon as you demand the hot water at a sink, shower, dishwasher or washing machine, the tankless hot water heater heats up the water passing through it. A tankless hot water heater can be electric, gas, or propane. Tankless water heaters are popular because they can cut your water-heating bill by 10 to 20 percent. The reason a tankless hot water heater saves you money is because it eliminates the need for the heat to be constantly running to keep the water hot "in-case" you need it. Instead, the tankless water heater only turns on when you need the hot water and other times it remains off. Another great thing about a tankless hot water heater is that with a regular hot water heater, you have a single large tank of hot water that was heated up. If you run a hot shower for too long, you can run out of water in your hot water heater until the new water is re-heated. However, with a tankless hot water heater, the water that comes through the heater is heated as you need it and never runs out because you are not relying on a single hot tank of water. One thing to know is that there are different sized on-demand hot water heaters. If you have a hot water radiant heat system in your house, a small tankless water heater may not be large enough and you may need to install an on-demand boiler (a larger version). In addition, you may even consider a bank up reservoir to store extra hot water so you don't run out while heating the house, running the dishwasher and taking a shower simultaneously which is common in a family household.

A summary of the reasons that tankless hot water heaters are becoming more and more popular today are described below:

- Tankless water heaters are compact in size. A tankless water heater will allow you to get rid of the large round hot water heater you have taking up space. A small residential tankless water heater is a small box that mounts to the wall and will allow you to expand your living area.

- Tankless water heaters eliminate the loss of energy wasted when hot water cools down in long pipes or while it's sitting in your typical hot water heater storage tank.

- Tankless hot water heaters provide warm water to the source quicker than standard hot water heaters. Therefore, less water is wasted because you do not have to let the water run as long to wait for the warm water to reach the faucet.

- Standard hot water heaters are susceptible to corrosion and have life expectancies of 7-12 years (because of water sitting in it for such a long period of time). The life of a tankless hot water heater is longer because water only passes through so it is less subject to corrosion. Tankless water heaters can last up to 20 years or more.

- The price of a tankless hot water heater is less than a standard hot water heater. So not only does it save water, take up less space and give you instant hot water, you can purchase them for less than a good hot water heater.

An on-demand tankless hot water heater is a great investment for a home. It is especially beneficial if you can create more useable space making a room larger or creating more storage space. Creating more space and making your home more efficient are two great ways to make your home more marketable. It can be done by replacing your standard hot water heater with a nice tankless hot water heater for less than $1,000.

Change the Filter in Your Air Conditioner.

If you have an air conditioner and your home has a stale musty smell when it is operating, you may need to change the filter in your air conditioning system. A major turn off for buyers is the potential for mold and mildew in a house. Don't let the smell of an old air conditioner filter fool buyers into thinking there is something much worse wrong with your home.

Go Green: Eco-friendly Homes Bring in a Higher Value

In this green conscious age, eco friendly upgrades have a large return on investment. There is a multitude of ways to make your home more eco friendly as I illustrate below including upgrading to water saving plumbing fixtures, upgrading to high efficiency appliances, choosing renewable resources such as bamboo for your flooring and other items that save on energy costs throughout the home. Replace as many materials as you can with green materials and strive to see if you can make your home a certified a green home.

A checklist is available at www.moveincertified.com. The creators of moveincertified.com have gotten together to create a green certification checklist with a point system to show potential buyers how green their home is (Class I or Class II). Below I highlighted some of the items on the list which I felt were the most attainable for a homeowner. The actual list is quite a bit longer and you can view in more detail on their website:

- There is an edible garden area
- The driveway is shared
- Drives and walkways are mostly of permeable material such as gravel
- Exterior Lighting is controlled by motion sensors
- Some of the outdoor/walkway lighting is solar powered
- There is south facing roof area for future solar use
- The roofing material is a light color in warm climates or a dark color in colder climates.
- The deck is made of composite recycled material
- Areas of potential air infiltration have been sealed, foamed or caulked
- The exterior doors have intact weather stripping
- The windows are mostly double glazed
- The windows are mostly low-e rated
- The crawlspace soil is covered by a vapor barrier

- The crawlspace is properly ventilated
- The furnace is centrally located
- The furnace filter is clean
- The furnace is at least 90% energy efficient or 80% for boilers
- A built-in electronic or HEPA air filter exists
- An in floor heating system exists
- A geothermal heating system exists
- The thermostat is programmable
- The heating/cooling system has more than one thermostat controlled zone
- No non-insulated ducts exist in outside walls
- No non-insulated ducts exist in the attic
- The water heater is high efficiency
- All hot water lines are insulated
- A tankless hot water heater exists
- The boiler has a side-arm water heater
- No faucets drip
- Kitchen and bath faucets have aerators
- All toilets are 1.6 gallons per flush or less
- A dual flush toilet(s) exist
- The attic is properly ventilated
- The home including attic is well insulated
- The refrigerator is rated for an annual electric cost of $66 or less
- Some light fixtures have dimmers
- Most fixtures are using compact fluorescent bulbs
- Recycled content or natural material (domestic cotton or wool) carpet is in use.
- There are no visible indications of lead
- There are no visible indications of asbestos
- There are no visible indications of mold

In this green modern age, eco conscious upgrades have a big return on investment. From water saving plumbing fixtures to tankless hot water heaters, investing in the earth can add value to your home. Choose rapidly renewable resources for finishes like bamboo flooring and opt for systems that save on energy costs. Regardless of the method, green living upgrades are always worth the investment. I just read an article that stated that of 1.6 million homes sold in California between the years of 2007 and 2012, holding all other variables constant, a green certification label on a house adds an average of 9 percent to the selling price.

Professionally Hardwire your Home for Telephone

Not all homes are hardwired with telephone lines. Many homes have telephone lines installed, but they typically only go to one or two locations in the home. Over the years, homeowners would route additional telephone wire to other locations in the home themselves by drilling holes and stapling phone cabling along baseboards over long distances. Even though over 70% of all people are using cellular lines over landlines today, it is still important to have landlines in your home for the following reasons:

Peace of Mind & Safety

Having a landline is important for 911 calls. While it is still possible to reach out to 911 operators with your cell phone, it may not be as quick for the operator to tell where you are located based on the GPS alone. A landline has several advantages over the cell phone in the following instances: If there are small children in a home that cannot relay their address accurately or if you are seriously injured and cannot speak to describe your location, the emergency operators can immediately get your location from your caller ID. During a major disaster your landline will be more reliable as cell phone lines may be jammed. Lastly, land lines offer access to emergency responders in rural areas where the cell phone is less than reliable.

In addition to the ability to call 911, parents find it wise to maintain a landline so babysitters have a dependable phone to make and receive calls in case of an emergency.

Reliability

If the power goes down in your neighborhood or home, your phone lines will still get a dial tone. For this reason, landlines provide homeowners with more security as they can stay in contact with people during times of emergency.

Working from home

The appeal of working from home is strong. Self employed people, moms with small kids or employees that have the ability to work independently from a remote office are all great candidates for doing most (if not all) of their regular work from a telecommuting arrangement. In most cases, a business person working from home does not want to hold a cell phone to their head to conduct business. Landlines are inexpensive with crystal-clear calling quality which is a requirement for a serious business person. In addition, someone may require a designated line for a fax machine. In this case, having telephone jacks hardwired to every room in the home is important.

Rural living

If your home is not close to any major cell phone towers, reception in a rural area will be poor. A cell phone will not be adequate for doing business or for day to day communication. Landlines hardwired directly to a phone company make much more sense.

Home security systems

Home security systems require a land line to communicate with emergency responders in case of break ins, fire or emergencies. There are other ways to make a home security system work, but most companies will not recommend those options when safety is of concern.

Clarity and less expensive than cellular phones

Traditional landline service plans are much less expensive than cell phone service plans and the clarity of a landline is typically better than using a cell phone.

While some might believe that landlines have become an old useless resource in the home, I have just shown you many reasons to keep it and to be sure your home is properly wired with phone lines. After learning the many reasons why landlines are important for a home, it is easy to see why having all the rooms of your home professionally hardwired with landlines is important. Someone looking at your home may be planning a home office, to purchase a security system or a family with children seeking a home with all possible safety features.

If your home is not already professionally wired with phone lines, I recommend installing outlets in each room of the house and having them hardwired internally through your walls, terminating in one central location where the phone company can connect directly from the telephone pole.

Professionally Hardwire your Home for Cable Television

Cable television is a system that transmits video services to subscribers by way of their cable operators via coaxial or optical fiber cables. In typical installations of cable television, your carrier of choice will come to your home and run a cable from the telephone pole to a specific location on your house. They connect a cable box to the side of your home unless you have a specified location inside your home that you wish them to connect too.

In many cases, older homes are not hardwired for cable. Meaning, homes do not have coaxial cable running internally through the walls from room to room with only cable outlets visible to hook up televisions to receive cable in multiple rooms. What this means is that the cable companies have to run and staple the cable wiring along the outside of your home along the siding. The cable company then drills entry points through your siding to enter the home at the locations you want your cable jacks such as the living room, recreation room and master bedroom.

The optimal situation is to have all rooms of your house hardwired with coaxial cable with cable outlets in each room. The coaxial wires from all of these locations would terminate at a single central location you choose in your house to control all of the cable. At this location, you would have a box with all of the coaxial wires coming into it. The cable company would hook your cable up to a router in this box and all of your rooms would have cable without having ugly wires stapled to the outside of your home and holes drilled into your siding.

Unless you have a lot of open crawl spaces in your home, hardwiring your home for cable television will cost some money because the wires will have to be fished through the walls by a professional electrician and brought to a single point of your choosing. The end result is a nice tidy system that will make the next cable hook up at your home a seamless and efficient experience for whomever gets to enjoy it.

Professionally Hardwire your Home for Internet

A home already wired for internet has its advantages. Similar to cable television wiring, it is important to have outlets in all rooms of the home for internet as well as cable and phone. There are wireless options for the internet, but most people who understand internet connections prefer wired over wireless.

Below are some reasons why your house should be wired for internet as opposed to relying on a wireless router:

Ease of use

Wired connections are easier to set up. With most computers today you can simply plug the cable jack into your computer and get onto the internet.

Reliability and speed

Cordless products are not as reliable as corded or wired products ever. Cordless products are likely to pick up interference and experience problems of quality. While wireless internet hardware has improved over the years, other electrical devices can still potentially interfere with your Internet, and in some cases causing disconnections and delays. Just like cordless phones, problems increase as you get farther away from the router.

Speed

Wired connections are always faster than wireless internet and never slower.

Security

The most important benefit of wired over wireless internet is your security level. A wired network is fully contained in your home. In order to connect to it, you must have physical access to the router as opposed to a wireless network which is not contained. Your neighbors and people outside your home can potentially find your network on their own computers and smart phones.

This is a concern for two reasons:

It is not difficult for a hacker to intercept data sent through an unsecured network. All of the banking, purchasing, and communication you do online could potentially be maliciously taken by an outsider. Identity theft and credit card fraud are just a couple of the potential hazards of using a wireless network at home.

You don't want people you don't know using your Internet connection. It'll be slower to you and any questionable actions they take online will be traced back to you, not to them.

As you can see, having your home wired for internet to each room is much better than relying on wireless. The process to wiring your home is similar to wiring for coaxial cable and phone lines. The wiring used is called Ethernet cable as opposed to coaxial cable which is used for cable. The goal is to NOT see any wiring. In the living spaces of your home, you only want to see outlets. All of the wiring should be internal through the walls and terminate at a single location of your choice in your home or garage. The company you purchase your internet through will connect to this single location in your house and you will use a router/switch to split the signal to all of the locations of your home. There is nothing worse than trying to clean dust balls and dirt out of clusters of data wires throughout the house.

If you can sell your home with internet already hardwired in, it will be selling point for many people that understand the benefits of wired versus wireless and maybe those who plan to work from home.

Complete Low voltage Wiring for Phone, Cable & Internet Combined

Low voltage wiring includes wiring for Audio, Video, Telephone, Intercom, Data, Alarm System, and generally any home wiring using less than 24 volts. In this case, I recommend having your home hardwired for cable, internet and phone together, all terminating at a single location in your home. Your phone company, cable company and internet service provider will hook up directly to this single location that you choose in your home or garage.

Professionally installing Low voltage wiring is a great way to add value to your home by making the electronic components in your home operate efficiently and with less hassle or mess.

As technology continues improving, it is increasingly necessary to have your house wired to accommodate this technology. It is more and more common in houses being built today to have a phone, cable and internet outlet in every single room in addition to multiple power outlets.

In addition, homes built today are often being wired to integrate computer networks, cable TV, and telephone all controlled through a central control panel typically located in a garage or utility room.

An older home without this amenity can be upgraded to include professionally hardwired low voltage wiring. In fact many homeowners are making these upgrades to their home and eliminating the strands of wires they have running along their baseboards collecting dust. Unfortunately, low voltage wiring is usually installed in new homes before insulation or drywall is installed, making it much easier and less expensive to route the wire. If you decide to install low voltage wiring into an existing finished home it can cost 5-10 times as much to retrofit the new wiring through the old closed up walls.

The value of your home will increase without a question by adding new low voltage wiring to your home. The home will become more attractive for future buyers and you will enjoy the upgrade as well over the duration of your final months in your home.

Install Fireplace

Adding a fireplace to a home can increase the value in two different ways. The first way adding a fireplace can increase your home value is by reducing energy consumption. The second way it increases for value is aesthetics and comfort.

A fireplace can either be a wood burning fireplace (most common in older homes), a pellet stove (usually a heat alternative, or a gas fireplace. Newer homes are being built with gas fireplaces. Older homes have wood burning fireplaces. While wood burning fireplaces are wonderful to have, they can be cumbersome because you have to have a large supply of wood and if you don't have a perfect set up or proper airflow, you can end up with quite a bit of smoke in your home. Gas fireplaces burn clean and the look and style of them has improved quite a bit over the last decade.

Reduces energy consumption

A fireplace can reduce the energy consumption in your home a few different ways. If you are using a wood burning fireplace or pellet stove, you can heat entire rooms or more with the fireplace and never need to turn on your heater (which either uses oil, electricity or gas). You can even save on your gas bill with a gas fireplace insert. The gas fireplace may produce more heat on the floor that you are on and eliminate the need for your furnace to turn on and heat the entire floor or home. As long as the family is in the room with the warm gas fireplace, there is no need to have the furnace kicking on and off over and over again.

Aesthetics & comfort

A fireplace can be a dramatic addition or centerpiece to a living space. Whether it is a living room, bedroom, kitchen or basement recreational room, a fireplace adds a comforting and eclectic feel that most other household improvements cannot compare too. There is something calming and primal about fire and the ability to contain its beauty and warmth within your home. Regardless of where you install it, a fireplace will light up a room and be a memorable feature for potential buyers as they explore homes they want to purchase.

If your home is located in a warm climate, a fireplace may not be the improvement to spend your money on. However, in colder climates, a fireplace is a must have; it heats up a room quickly and is beautiful to look at.

Upgrade Fireplace

If your home already has a wood burning fire place, then you may want to consider these two ideas to improve your existing fireplace.

Change the look:

One thing I have noticed over the years is that many fireplaces are dated and not very pleasant to look at (they contain really bad fake wood, foggy glass, etc.). The reason they usually stay the same over the years is because they are surrounded by stone, brick or tile and most people don't want to mess with these types of materials. So over the years the walls evolve and get wall paper, then painted, then textured, then painted again and the fireplace stays constant. A fireplace does not have to stay the same. A fireplace can be modernized or rejuvenate to match the current style and color palette of your home. The easiest thing you can do it paint the fireplace. It seems strange painting stone, brick and tile, but changing it to a color that matches your interior décor will look ten times better than the ugly tile or stone that you forced yourself to cope with over the years. I recently had a situation in my own house where we had the original tile around the fireplace in a 1920's home that I bought to live in. The tile was a very unattractive original batchelder tile. We lived with the ugly tile for over a year because it was original to the home and the thought of painting it seemed sinful. Then one day we decided we couldn't take it any longer. We painted the tile Navajo White, which was the same color as all the millwork in the house. All of a sudden this big old fireplace became a wonderful blended part of the décor versus an elephant in the room.

Another way to change the look of the fireplace is by changing the mantle. You can change the wood on it, get rid of it, raise it or lower it. Another thing people do is re-frame a new front to the fireplace. A new fireplace surround can be framed and drywalled or covered in hardi-panels to create a unique or contemporary looking fireplace. Framing a new front on an old fireplace is great because you can preserve the original fireplace behind the framing in case a future buyer of your home wants to revert it back to its original form. Once you have re-framed the fireplace with your own style, you can paint it any color you want and enjoy it.

Upgrade to gas:

The greatest way to improve your wood burning fireplace while also increasing the value of your home is to install a gas fireplace insert. Almost all new homes include a gas fireplace. A gas fireplace will give you real flames and heat at the flick of a switch without the smoke and hassle of lighting a fire. How many times have you gotten nestled in for the night, ready to watch TV. and eat some food. You place the logs in the fireplace and get the fire started. Ten minutes later, everyone is choking in your living room because half of the smoke is coming into your home versus up the chimney. Wood burning fireplaces do not work well and in many cases make your house smell like a campsite. Besides the fact that someone has to chop or buy the wood, you have to have something to light the wood with and someone has to clean the fire place of it ashes and the half burnt wood. Overall the experience can be a negative one. People today prefer to flick a switch and enjoy a fire. If you live in a colder climate that has harsh winters, gas inserts today give off enough heat to heat most of your house. When seeking out gas fireplace inserts, you have the option to purchase one that has blowers to blow the heat into the house as well as the amount of heat they give off depending upon the size (square feet) of the room you are trying to heat. The last great point about a gas fireplace is that they have come a long way in the last decade and now appear more realistic than ever. We have all seen some terrible gas fireplaces over the years. I recently bought one and was blown away by the realness of the logs and embers inside. The cost to install a gas fireplace insert can range from $2500-$4000 depending upon how much heat you are seeking from the unit and the size of your fireplace opening.

Install Solar Tubes

Solar tubes are cylinders used to bring natural light into homes to add light while reducing electrical costs. They are common in hallways, sun rooms, walk-in closets and bathrooms. I have to admit that when I saw the solar tubes in the store, I didn't think I would ever like them. I thought solar tubes were the poor man's skylight. A year later I was in a friend's newly remodeled house and he showed me his new bathroom. The bathroom was very bright. I thought the lights were on, but they weren't. The light was coming from the Solar tube he had installed during his bath remodel. I was very impressed with the brightness and modern look of the Solar tub. Solar tubes are a great alternative to skylights because skylights are hard to install in most pre-built homes due to their size (2 feet by 4 feet, 4 feet by 4 feet and larger). In addition to the difficulty in installing skylights, you may not get the same amount of light unless the sun is at the right angle and there are absolutely no clouds in the sky. Skylights don't always illuminate as well as a solar tube because a solar tube uses smart technology which takes skylights one step further by refracting, reflecting and concentrating solar light through a small tube and into your space using mirrors and lenses

Install Skylights

Skylights can make a dramatic improvement to any room if you have a pitched roof anywhere in your house. Skylights need to be professionally installed so they don't leak water when it rains. Skylights come in all different shapes and sizes. Some skylights open to let in fresh air while most are permanently shut.

Skylights create a more energy efficient home because you will use less electricity lighting your home with the use of skylights. A skylight is a large window installed in the ceiling that will provide lots of light resulting in less usage of electricity to light your room. Sunlight equates to heat. Because skylights let in large amounts of sunlight, you may also be able to decrease the amount of energy you use to heat the room in the winter in addition to the energy savings on your lights.

Skylights will add value to a home by creating drama and depth to your rooms. If you install a large skylight, it will open up your room and make it seem bigger and brighter. Smaller skylights, which are great for additional lighting in halls, pantries, closets, or other obscure areas, also give your home a more modern look from the outside.

State of the art Audio and Sound:

Since most buyers are in search of a turnkey home, it means they do not intend to open up the walls to add amenities they desire.

One of these amenities that has been very popular in higher priced homes is built in sound systems and wiring.

When installing a sound system in your home, you begin by choosing a central location in the house to house the receivers, wire hubs, power and other audio equipment. From this point you run your speaker and other essential audio wiring through the walls, floors or ceilings to the desired locations. You can install and hardwire in speakers, or it is almost just as impressive to have speaker jack outlets in common speaker location in different rooms to allow the user to place their own speakers throughout the home.

If you wire in speakers do different locations in your home, you should also consider selling the house with the audio equipment so that the audio system is fully functioning for the buyer upon closing. The master control room would have the receiver with an iPod docking station. Then each room of your house could have speakers built into the walls or ceiling which can be controlled by a volume dial in each room. Music can be piped through the entire house. A house equipped with a full state of the art sound system will give your home a technological boost above the competitors; especially if you include the audio equipment with the house.

Lastly, if you have a media or movie room, plan accordingly with your audio installation. Be sure the buyer will have speaker jacks on the walls in proper locations, including a subwoofer outlet, that all route back to a control room where the new owner can place their movie equipment. If you want to take this a step further, you may consider purchasing and mounting a flat screen TV., speakers and receiver to complete the theater and offer with the house as a theater package. Large flat screen TV's have gone down in price from $2,000 to $600. You could install a TV., receiver and blue ray DVD player for less than $1,000 and put your home ahead of the competition. It is incredible how something is simple as a $1,000 movie theatre bundle gift may close a buyer on your house.

Ceiling Fans

While you might not think it, ceiling fans can add a tasteful element to any room in your house. When using a ceiling fan in lieu of air conditioning, a ceiling fan will dramatically reduce utilities costs. Using a ceiling fan to circulate warm air in the winter will also help reduce the heating bills. In addition to the potential cost savings on your utility bills, ceiling fans enhance a room's aesthetic and can add additional lighting. Many people prefer a ceiling fan in the bedroom.

Installing a ceiling fan in your home can make a big impact in the atmosphere at a low cost while cutting the home owner's expenses. Before buying ceiling fan, you should know which area of the house it will be installed and determine the size and style of fan that you will need. Usually, you will see in most homes that the fan is installed in the middle of the room.

Choosing the right ceiling fan is important to maximize its potential in your home. They play an important role of keeping us cool in the summer by cooling the temperatures of our rooms and blowing wind which helps us drain out most of the heat. Ceiling fans are something that we use every day in our life but do not give much consideration.

Once you begin your search for ceilings fans, you will quickly learn that the decision is not as simple as you might have expected. Ceiling fans are offered in a variety of different styles, sizes and prices. They begin at a very generic level and the costs increases as you increase the style and quality factor in addition to added features such as lights.

A ceiling fan is not going to add a lot of value to your home, but it definitely adds to the overall appeal to the home if placed somewhere that makes a lot of sense. Ceiling fans are more common and more desired in a warmer climate.

Add Air Conditioning / Central Air

Air conditioning is a great value added feature of a home where the outdoor temperate exceeds 75 to 80 degrees for long periods of time throughout the year. Air conditioning is even more necessary in these same regions that experience high amounts of humidity, which makes it feel even warmer than it actually is. The price for air conditioning can vary greatly depending upon whether you currently have ducting in place for a heating system or old air conditioning system. The ducting has to be done properly so you do not build-up condensation and mold.

Air conditioning and central air systems will increase the value of your home. Potential buyers will undoubtedly consider a home with air conditioning over a home without. A home with air conditioning is a luxury that will give peace of mind to a family knowing they will not be suffering in the summer months ahead in your home as opposed to the competing homes on the market without AC. Buyers are looking for more than just the number of bedrooms and bathrooms. They are seeking comfort amenities both inside and outside including the type of heat, whether your home has air conditioning, etc.

Add a Water Filtration System

Installing a water filtration system in your home will improve the value of your house in that it will save money for future home owners.

You can install a water filtration system right in the kitchen with a tap that serves up fresh clean water. Another option is to upgrade to a refrigerator that has a water filtration system in it.

Creating a money saving luxury will give value to potential home owners. Future home owners will not have to buy purified water from the store any more therefore saving money.

Small luxuries like this add up in the eyes of a buyer. All the little details you can add that improve someone's life are noted in buyer's heads as they preview different homes in their search.

Clear Out Unfinished Crawl Spaces

You are going to have to do this eventually, so you might as well do it now. Clear all of your personal belongings and undesirables out of the storage areas. Clear out the crawl spaces and strange triangular closets beneath the staircases, etc. so that the full size of the space can be seen and appreciated. People love storage and will want to see the space empty so they can imagine their own belongings (holiday storage items, photo albums, etc.) stored in these spaces. Clear them out, clean them up and add light if they don't have any so the potential can be seen.

De-Clutter Interior

I have mentioned removing items from storage and crawl spaces, in addition to objects obstructing light from windows and debris outdoors and on your roof. However, an important and basic improvement which will make your home appear to be more valuable is the simple de-cluttering of your rooms before photos or allowing any showings. You may have seen this over and over again on home and real estate television shows. Real estate experts always recommend painting in light neutral tones and always the removal of clutter. Buyers will have a hard time conceptualizing your space if it is full of your personal belongings. You must be able to see the floor, walls and table tops. Be sure there is space to breath and room to move. Remove collections, magazines, extra seating, pillows, blankets, pictures and more. Remove as many personal items as possible until your rooms become spacious. Everyone has different taste. Remove your personality from your home interior so other people can imagine themselves in your home easier. Sometimes people think buyers can see through the clutter. The truth is, most people cannot see through the clutter. You need to do the work for them. Clear out your spaces as best you can and make it easy for buyers to envision themselves in your home and inspire offers. What this basically means is that you need to start moving out of your home before you sell. This is a difficult concept for many people because a lot of sellers wait to sell the house before they move. However, what if a home won't sell until you remove your personal items and clutter? It is a commitment some home owners need to make in order for a successful sale to occur.

Turn Crawl Space into Useable Space

In this book we talk about removing personal items from storage spaces and crawl spaces that are already useable. But, how about the crawl spaces that are still uninhabitable? Almost all houses have spaces that only contain framing, insulation or loose boards. By converting these spaces into useable storage spaces, you will create a more versatile, useful and appealing home. Everyone needs a place to put boxes of memorabilia, holiday decorations and other storage items.

For a crawl space or attic space to be useable as storage space, it must be dry, safe and have a sturdy floor.

For crawl spaces beneath the house, the floor must be concrete, wood or some sort of vapor barrier to protect the bottom of your boxes and storage items from moisture. The space must be clean, well lit and easily accessible.

For attic spaces, with bare floor joists, you must first create a solid floor with some sort of sheeting such as plywood or OSB. If you have insulated walls or ceilings in this space, it is a good idea to sheet them with drywall to protect yourself and your belongings from fragments of insulation that will undoubtedly fall on to you and your belongings as you come and go from the space. In addition to the walls and a floor, keep in mind that you will want some sort of light (typically fluorescent light is the appropriate and safe light type for closets and storage spaces). Some people may also wish to dress up the entrance to the space with a nice door including trim. Just because the space is storage space, doesn't mean it has to have a dingy door to enter. This new space is important space and should have the same quality and workmanship as the other features of your home.

Convert Unfinished Basement into Livable Space

The unfinished basement is a hidden treasure. When I buy a home to remodel, the basement is one of the first places I look for hidden potential. A basement converted into a living space will dramatically improve the value of a home. If you obtain permits and construct the remodel to code, you will add finished square feet to your home which will absolutely increase the home value. Since we know that finishing a basement will increase your home value, the important challenge is to be sure that the resulting increase in value will be greater than the cost of the improvement.

Below are some factors to consider in planning your basement remodel:

Seek out hidden potential

- Are your basement ceilings high enough to turn the basement into a livable space that would allow the average height person to walk about comfortably?
- Can you add a bathroom or create a full bath from a half bath?
- Can you add one to two bathrooms?
- Do you have enough natural light?
- Can you add a movie theater, entertainment bar or studio?
- Can you create a large comfortable living space?

Getting going:

If you have said yes to one or more of the above questions, you should definitely consider moving forward with the improvement.

- Draw up a basic plan of how you want to layout the basement (with assistance from experienced friends and contractors)
- Obtain bids from contractors

- Obtain permits
- Begin

Some tips and ideas for your basement remodel:

- Install recessed can lights throughout. Your ceilings will be too low for you to use any other type of light. Sconces are another possibility.
- You can create larger rooms by installing large supporting beams and headers in places of supporting walls.
- On the flip side, if you see a large open space, don't be afraid to chop it up to create a bedroom or bath.
- Create a well planned kitchen and bath layout. The kitchen and bath should be close to each other or back to back since they share the same water source and drains.
- Ceiling Obstacles: If you have low pipes such as drain pipes, water lines, electrical wires or ductwork, make every effort to re-route the utilities through the floor joists if possible. A lot of times, prior contractors will run pipes and wires beneath the floor joists if the basement is not a living area. After multiple upgrades to piping and electrical, the basement ceiling can look pretty sloppy. Now that you are converting this unused space into a livable space, those utilities need to be cleaned up and buried in the ceiling so your ceiling can be max height. If you cannot move or replace any of the pipes and wires, your only choice is to have them boxed in and drywalled when the ceiling is framed up and drywalled. The downside to this is that it will make your basement ceiling lower than you want. The ultimate goal of a good basement remodel is to make your basement not feel like a basement. You typically do not have anything obstructing your headroom on the 1st or 2nd floor of a house, so try not to have anything obstructing your headroom in the basement if it can be done.
- Make for darn sure it will not flood! I don't need to tell you how important this is. First, be sure that the

downspouts on the outside of the house are clear and route all of the roof water away from the house. I found that poorly installed or lack of downspouts are the main reason for flooding in basements. Consider installing a French drain. A French drain can be installed around the border of the outside of your house or they can also be installed along the interior boarder of your basement wall. Another thing to check are your water sources on the 1st floor. Is there a kitchen sink, toilet, shower, bathtub or washing machine on the floor above your future finished basement? As you are well aware, all of these fixtures flood from time to time. Create some safety measures such as access doors in the ceiling beneath certain appliances in case you need to make a repair from below or in case of dripping from an above sink or tub. You can caulk the edge of the bathroom floor or laundry room floor to slow down any future flooding into the basement. You can buy a large tray for your washing machine that will catch any flooding water and discharge it into your drain pipe (available at home improvement stores) and lastly, you can purchase small alarms that sit on the floor next to your appliance and the alarm will sound if water floats beneath it connecting two metal points together.

- Is your furnace or hot water heater in the middle of the basement? There are two options if your furnace and/or hot water heater are in the way: You can build around them, leaving plenty of room and access doors to get to the appliances for future repairs, replacement and proper venting (this means your basement living space will be built in a circle versus a large open space). The other option, which I like best, is to move the furnace or hot water heater to a wall if possible and extending your ductwork, electrical or plumbing lines to the new locations. For gas appliances, you will need to create new venting, which shouldn't be difficult or expensive if you are moving the appliance closer to an exterior wall. Moving the furnace or hot water heater out of the center of the basement opens up your space dramatically so you can divide it up the way you like versus designing a great living space around the appliances.

- Give yourself plenty of lighting, electrical outlets and heat.

- Windows: Replace old single pane windows with some new double pane windows that slide open for fresh air. New windows offer more light, insulation and security over the original single pane windows that most old basements have.

- If you think that adding a mother in law apartment would be a marketable feature to have in your neighborhood, then now is the time to create this. Be sure there is separate access for your tenant to come and go, a decent kitchen, bath and possibly laundry. If you will be renting out the unit, there will be very specific safety codes and permits to be aware of and apply for. If you ignore the codes and a neighbor reports you to the city, you will spend a considerable sum of money changing the mother-in-law apartment back to a generic living space.

- If you plan to make a movie theater I have a tip for you: Pre-wire the walls for speakers so that you can have all of your auxiliary items in one spot. You can buy the speaker wire outlet boxes from the hardware store. Then run wires from your auxiliary area to where speakers will go. You will have outlet boxes where the speakers will be. After you drywall, there are special outlet covers you will put on these boxes that will look like professional speak boxes with a left and a right jack for your speakers. Don't forget a wire for your sub-woofer. While doing this, don't forget rear speakers for the walls or ceiling. Another detail I have done is to run some drainage pipe (ABS pipe) or conduit through the ceiling and walls so that if I need to run wires to a future projector or video screen, I can simply push the wires through the pipe that is already embedded in the wall without any future drilling or patching of drywall.

- Flooring: I suggest that if you install carpeting to use a good rubber padding. In addition to carpet, you should consider a hard surface such as tile or vinyl at the entrances so your carpet does get ruined from dirt being tracked in. In addition, if you install a bar, bath, kitchen or laundry room, your floor should also be hard for easy clean up.

- Paint: If you are creating a movie theater, the experts use a dark matte paint. Matte paint will not reflect the light from your TV or movie screen which makes the viewing experience more true to movie theaters. Light reflecting off the walls will actually reflect back onto your movie screen and wash out the crispness of your image.

Add an Entertainment Bar

What home is complete without a place to entertain? A well appointed entertainment bar in a living room, basement or man cave can make a great addition to a home. Several options for bars include store bought bars or custom made bars.

Store bought bars are similar to kitchen islands. You can find brand new bars at furniture stores to match your style whether contemporary or classic. These bars usually have drawers for your bar accessories and storage for glasses and bottles. You can also find fantastic second hand bars at antique and consignment stores if you are looking for a unique older piece to match a specific style.

Custom made bars are typically made of a combination of kitchen cabinetry, a countertop and a sink. This type of bar can be built into a wall or as an island with all four sides finished.

Either way you create your bar, be sure that it is consistent with the style of your interior design and furnishings. If your furniture is antique, 60's modern or contemporary, try to match the style so that the entertainment bar appears as though it has always been there.

Create Rentable Space: Income Producing Mother-In-Law Unit

Creating rentable space is one of my favorite improvements to a home because it essentially increases the number of home buyers that can afford to purchase your home. To explain, if you have a home that is out of the average buyer's price range, adding an income producing feature to the home essentially makes your home more affordable as the rental income will cover the larger mortgage that would normally out of their comfort zone. Your home may be $80,000 over someone's budget, but if you create a 1 bedroom apartment that can bring in $800.00/month, then that $80,000 price increase to purchase your home becomes null and void to the buyer that previously would not have been able to afford your home. In some cases, a mortgage lender may even consider the potential rental income towards the buyer's income which will allow the buyer to qualify for the larger mortgage to buy your home. It becomes a win win situation for both the buyer and the seller. For the buyer, your income producing feature is an opportunity to purchase a better, higher valued home than they could normally afford and for the seller, it is the opportunity to sell to a broader audience of buyers.

A rental space can be created out of a basement, a solid garage, outbuilding or in some cases a top floor or first floor. Check the laws in your State and you might be surprised about how flexible the laws are for having a mother-in-law apartment on your property. These laws differ from State to State and city to city. Some cities are more flexible than others. Regardless of how flexible your city is on allowing mother-in-law units, you will still have building and fire codes to adhere to so that your new space is safe and rentable for tenants. Most laws are put into place to ensure that an occupant living in your space will be able to escape in case of fire or flooding. The laws are meant to protect your tenants as well as protecting you from being liable for something catastrophic happening to your tenant.

If you have tall ceilings in your basement and a separate entrance, the basement makes the best income producing rental. I have seen garages turned into wonderful one bedroom apartments as well.

Section 2

Exterior Improvements

Paint Exterior

Painting the exterior of your home is one of the greatest improvements you can make to your home prior to selling. A fresh coat of paint on the exterior of your home will immediately increase the value of your home while making a huge impression on home buyers.

Depending upon whether your home needs a simple repaint or a complete restoration and repaint, the price for a good exterior paint job with vary from $3000 (prime & paint) to $20,000 (full restoration). If you do not need to restore your siding with hours of scraping, sanding, bondo, caulk and wood putty, then you might be able to execute these major improvements for a low cost of around $3500 - $5000. An exterior paint job is one of the most cost effective improvements that you can do to increase the chances of a quicker sell while also adding more value to your house.

Studies have shown that repainting the exterior of your home can add up to 10% in the resale value of your house.

The appearance of your home on the outside is the deciding factor whether or not the potential buyer will look at your home on the inside.

Just as when you are painting your interior, it is best to use neutral (whites, creams, tan, etc.), fresh colors that complement each other and just as importantly blends in with the rest of your neighborhood. Neutral paint colors will appeal to the greatest number of people.

Wherever you decide to purchase your paint, the paint manufacturers usually provide helpful brochures which include paint color schemes for your home exterior. These brochures can be very helpful for obtaining neutral color schemes and combinations for your home's exterior. If you are seeking additional assistance besides driving around the neighborhood for inspiration, take a look at the painter manufacturer's brochures for their professional paint color combination ideas.

Build a Deck

Building a deck can make a dramatic difference to your home. Would your home be more enjoyable with a large or small deck off the back door? If a deck would be perfect for enjoying the back or front yard of your home then you should consider installing one. The costs can vary but it does not have to be an expensive improvement. You have a lot of control over costs. If cost is an issue, you can save money by adjusting the style of your railings or perhaps no railings at all if your deck is only a couple feet off the ground. A deck makes a great transition from your home to the yard. It is a great place to grill out and enjoy friends & family. A deck doesn't have to be large. You can have a moderately sized deck built in the price range of $1,200 - $2,000 depending on its size, height and railing style. If you have a large intricate deck, or one that is high off the ground, the cost will greatly increase. Overall, you will find that the expense is mostly in the labor and less in the materials. Even with the price of lumber constantly increasing, it seems as though the cost of all the materials to build a deck is always surprisingly low unless you choose specialty lumber.

The materials you use can greatly affect the cost of your deck. The most common material is pressure treated wood and cedar. If you want a deck that will never need to be treated or refinished, Trex® is a wood alternative that comes in all different shapes and sizes. Trex® is more expensive than real wood, but it lasts longer. The color and style options were not great at first, but as this company has grown, their selection and likeness to real wood has improved a lot making this a very popular product to build decks out of.

Refinish Deck and Seal to Protect

Make your deck bright and fabulous again by having it refinished. This home improvement idea is near and dear to my heart because I used to own and operate my own deck waterproofing and refinishing company. I enjoyed doing this work because the results were so rewarding. Unless the deck is too far gone and rotted, cleaning and staining a deck has shocking results. Homeowners are always surprised at the renewed look of their deck after a professional refinishing. The dark, dirty and moldy wood you see is only on the surface. Wood is very resilient and beyond the surface is the original golden or red wood that once gleamed with newness. You can usually get that color back.

Here is how it is done:

If you don't own a pressure washer, head to your local home improvement store or equipment rental store and rent a pressure washer. Be sure to get a pressure washer with a PSI (pressure per square inch) range of 1500 – 2500 and a GPM (gallons per minute) over 4. Getting a pressure washer with these numbers will ensure results. Hook the pressure washer up to a good water source and begin washing every inch of your deck, posts and railings. If you have never used a pressure washer before on wood, please consult a professional before beginning the process so you do not destroy the wood. A good pressure washer will do a fabulous job, but it can also rip through your wood causing a lot of damage and leaving marks. The pressure washer will come with 2-4 different tips for your spray gun. I would recommend a 40-45 degree tip which will give you a 3-4 inch fan of powerful spray. If you are using a lower PSI pressure washer, then you may prefer the 25 degree tip better because it will create more force than the 40-45 degree tip to compensate for the less powerful pressure washer. Wash the deck flooring and railing. Wash all four sides of every railing post. Do not leave a spot unclean. Be sure to get the outside of the deck including the posts, sides and anything visible from the street or yard. Something to note is that even though I became really good with a pressure washer, I still made the wood fuzzy and slightly splintery at times. Some people don't believe in pressure washing decks because it makes the wood fuzzy. It is fuzzy because you are essentially spraying a thin layer of the surface off the wood and exposing fresh wood. If this potential issue bothers you, there are products you can buy that will clean old deck wood, but it will not come close to the results of a pressure washer. You cannot really sand a deck because of the screw or nail heads. Pressure washing your deck will remove the grey and black layer of dirt, moss, mold and sun damaged wood. The results should be a yellow or golden, almost new looking wood (with a little fuzz on it).

Once the deck and railings are cleaned, give it 1-3 days to dry in the sun before you apply any sort of stain or sealant. Even though the surface appears dry, you want the wood to be thoroughly dry so the sealant or stain you apply will absorb correctly. A clear sealant alone will look great on your newly washed deck. However, if you want to make it even better, there are deck waterproofing products that are lightly tinted/stained which will ad a touch of color to your newly refinished deck. A common brand that I like is CWF (Clear Wood Finish). This product has a clear finish, in addition to a reddish cedar finish and many more color options. CWF needs to be rolled and brushed onto the deck. There are lighter/thinner products on the market that can be sprayed onto the deck with a pump sprayer such as Thompsons Water Seal. This looks great too. If you use a pump sprayer to apply sealant to your deck, be sure to tarp off the surrounding area to product your lawn, plants and more from the airborne chemicals.

Your deck and railings should look like new depending on the condition and age of your deck. During this process of cleaning and refinishing, it is a good idea to replace any rotting floor boards or railing pieces. If needed, replace boards before you stain so that you can blend the new pieces in with the old using your color tinted sealant.

One important note on staining or painting your deck: I highly recommend you stay away from solid stains or paints on your deck. No matter what the label says, there is no flooring paint that can withstand weather and people walking on a deck. The result will be chipping and scratching of the paint and stain on the high traffic areas. If your deck is not already painted with a solid paint or stain, be sure to use a transparent (completely see through) or semi-transparent (see through with a touch of color) stain to colorize your deck. My personal recommendation is to stay away from solid stain or paint unless the deck or railings were already painted. Once painted with a solid color, there is no turning back unless you want to strip the paint off with chemicals and this will become a much larger job than you will want to pursue.

Your newly refinished deck will surely turn heads and put your home a step above the rest as most home owners ignore and let erode, this very important feature of their home. I don't think it is laziness as much as it is that most people don't realize that the deck can be refinished for such a low cost.

Gutters

One of the most important functional features of any house is the gutters. The gutters and downspouts have to be fully functional to protect the home. Several issues to be aware of as a homeowner: Are the gutters leaking at any seams? Are there downspouts? Is the roof water being directed away from the house at the bottom of the downspouts? Are the gutters catching all of the water that comes off the roof? There are all very important factors in determining the current state of your gutters. Most often than none, when a basement or crawl space of a house floods, it is due mainly to bad gutters or downspouts (downspouts don't exist or they were not installed properly to direct water away from the house as intended).

Have your gutters repaired if you notice water dripping at the seams or corners where they connect. Add downspouts where needed and properly direct the water as needed. Be sure that if your down spouts are connected to the storm drain pipes that the pipes are clear of debris so they actually work. You will be surprised at how inexpensive it is to have your gutters fixed or replaced. Most companies will pull up in a trucked with equipment that makes seamless gutters and can replace everything on the spot without any trips to the hardware store. In fact, if you have bent and leaky gutters on your entire house, you may consider replacing them in their entirety because it may only be $400-$800 to replace them all. Note that plastic gutters (gutters you purchase at home improvement stores) usually leak a lot and should be replaced with metal gutters with minimal seems. Plastic gutters can be bought and installed by homeowners and typically need to be replaced in a short time because of their poor performance. Gutters are not something that you want to cut corners on because when they are faulty, it could cost you thousands of dollars to replace carpet, drywall and furniture in the lower levels of your house due to flooding. Other things that can be damaged by cheap or faulty gutters are the siding and window trim beneath the gutters that gets damaged from constant dripping or water flow throughout the different seasons.

Gutter Aesthetics: Most people don't think about this, but gutters come in different colors. You may choose to change the color of your gutters from white to brown or brown to black. This can all be done. In addition to newer metal gutters with clean straight lines, you can replace downspouts with downspout chains and bells. These chain and bell downspouts give your home a unique look and feel. These bells and chains serve the same purpose of a downspout and actually work despite how they look. They are very interesting looking and can quickly spruce up the front of a house.

Rain Barrel

Some buyers will think a rain barrel is a fantastic addition to a home because it conserves water and reduces the utility cost of the home. A rain barrel is a large plastic barrel that can be purchased from most home improvement stores and plant nurseries. The barrel can be purchased for a very reasonable cost (approximately $100+) and installed by the homeowner. The rain barrel gets installed at the base of one of your downspouts. The downspout which normally routes the water collected in your gutters to proper drainage is rerouted into the rain barrel. The rain barrel eventually fills up with water and the excess water gets redirected to wherever your downspout was already sending the rain water from your gutters. The rain barrel creates a reserve of water that can be used to water the grass and garden. Rain barrels have a on / off valve at the bottom of them which you can hook a garden hose up to. The pressure of the full barrel of water creates enough force for the water to come through the hose to water your lawn, garden or fill up buckets to clean your cars. A rain barrel is not for everyone, but there is a sector of people that will love that you have it as long as you can find an area to install the rain barrel that does not detract from your curb appeal.

Repair or Replace Roof

I highly recommend that you don't try selling a house with a leaky roof or one with different colored patches. A roof will always get called out in an inspection and you will ultimately have to fix it, replace it or reduce your sales price to appease the buyer. With this in mind, you should be sure your roof is in great shape so that inspectors don't target the roof in an inspection. In addition to have a functioning roof in great condition, the appearance of the roof has a lot to do with the value of your home.

If you can fix or patch the roof while keeping the appearance completely uniform then you will save quite a bit of money. However, if you believe it is necessary to replace your roof, some key considerations are the type of material, style, color and cost. There are many different types of roofing materials available to choose from.

Asphalt shingles

Approximately 80% of all United States roofs have asphalt shingles due to its low cost, ease of installation, and resiliency to the different seasons. These shingles are the flat tar shingles that have a rough sandy surface. Asphalt shingles come in a huge variety of colors, longevity options, and price points. These shingles are your least expensive option for your roof, but they have the worst environmental track record. Asphalt shingles have a low insulation value and a shorter lifespan than many other roofing materials available today. Asphalt shingles are not usually recyclable because of the layer of fiberglass added to the shingles and because they are made from petroleum products.

Wood shingles and shakes

Wood shingles or shakes are a chunky wood shingled roof common on ranches houses, cottages, bungalows and certain historic homes. Wood shingles and shakes can be purchased in redwood, cedar, southern pine and other woods, cedar being the most costly. The difference between wood shingles and wood shake is that wood shingles are cut by a machine, while wood shakes are handmade which gives them an even rougher look. Wood shingles and shake roofs may or may not be fire retardant, so be sure to check the rating if it is a concern. Wood shingles and shake roofs last longer than asphalt shingles and can last longer, but can be a lot more expensive.

Wood shingles and shakes have a synthetic alternative made from plastic, rubber and mixed recycled wood. These synthetic shingle and shake roofs are light weight, UV-resistant, fire-resistant, and long lasting. These synthetic roofs can have a lifespan up to 50-years.

Clay & concrete tiles

Another type of roof is Clay tile roofing. Clay tiles are very heavy and require additional roof framing. Clay tile roofs are common on homes in warmer climates and can be seen on Santa Fe, Mediterranean and Spanish style homes. These roofs are non-combustible and extremely durable. The tiles come in many different hues, shapes, textures and styles that they don't even look like tiles at all.

Slate

Slate has a beautiful, distinctive appearance. Slate is very heavy and will also require additional framing similar to clay tiles.

A slate roof will last for hundreds of years. It is easy to repair and recyclable. Slate roofs are not recommended for high-heat locations due to its dark color / absorption of heat. Slate roofs are common on Colonial, French, and Chateau style homes.

Metal (steel, aluminum, tile and copper)

Metal roofs are available in copper, aluminum, and stainless steel, and often have a high percentage of recycled content. They offer high insulation solar reflectance, and durability, often lasting twice as long as wood or asphalt. Metal roofing comes in different styles. Metal shingles typically simulate traditional roof coverings, such as wood shakes, shingles, slate and tile. On a side note, I bought an old home with metal roof shingles and had to replace the roof. My home had water stained walls due to the failures of this metal shingle roof. The only good thing about the roof was that when we tore it off, we were able to exchange it for cash at a recycling station. Other common types of metal roofing that you see often on homes and barns are the metal roofs with long straight vertical ridges from the top of the roof to the bottom. This has become a more popular roof in modern homes and remodels. Metal roofs are much lighter than most materials and very resistance to adverse weather (as long as it is installed perfectly). Common on Bungalow, ranch, contemporary and cottage style homes.

If you end up replacing your roof, you are most likely going to replace it with the materials that were originally on it. However, now that you know about the variety of roofing materials, you may want to consider an upgrade of the materials to give your home an edge over the competition.

Clean the Roof of Debris

If your home is surrounded by trees and has tree limbs higher than the roof line, chances are you have leaves, branches, sticks, seeds and/or pine needles on your roof or in the gutters. Before you photograph and/or list your house for sale, you should clean the roof of any and all debris. If the pitch of your roof is not very steep, you may be able to do this yourself. Grab a ladder and use a broom to remove leaves, sticks, and other debris. Once all of the large debris have been removed, use a garden hose to spray-clean the roof, gutters and downspouts. Needless to say, spraying water on your roof will make it very slippery and dangerous, so be very careful.

If you have moss growing on your roof, you will want to remove this too. There are several ways to remove moss from your room. The best way to remove the moss is by hand because pressure washing can destroy your roof. Never use a pressure wash to clean your roof unless you have wood shingles, clay, slate or concrete. Even with these other roofing materials, you still need to proceed with caution and spray downwards and not upwards so you do not blow off the roofing tiles or spray water beneath them. Another option to remove mold is to treat the moss with a moss killer that you can purchase at a hardware store. Some moss killers come in the form of powder while others come in the form of liquid that attaches to the end of your hose. You spray the roof with the moss killer and within a week or so; the moss is supposed to die, loosen up and fall off the roof. I suggest getting back up on the roof and sweeping it off and making sure your gutters do not fill up with moss and dirt.

If you are not comfortable getting up on your roof, hire a professional to clean the debris and/or moss. The roof protects everything that we call home. Because it is such an expensive item to replace, a clean roof free of debris and mold will make your home more attractive to buyers.

Siding Replacement or Repair

Siding is not a common item to replace when selling a home. Replacing siding is usually something you do when you purchase a fixer at a good price because it can be costly (over $10,000 easily). Most people might opt to fix or repair siding. However, if your home has the worst siding in the neighborhood, then the money you invest into replacing your siding could come back twofold. Below I describe the different types of siding options available for most homes.

Aluminum or vinyl siding

Aluminum and vinyl siding is available for newer homes, but most often found on older homes. This type of siding typically covers up old siding in need of restoration. In many cases with vinyl and aluminum siding, instead of repainting old wood siding, people were sold on the idea of re-siding over the original wood siding with vinyl or aluminum. The biggest advantage of this type of siding is that they do not require painting. The disadvantage is that aluminum siding dents and vinyl siding fades & cracks. Vinyl siding has improved over time as the quality of vinyl improves. Vinyl and aluminum siding have a cheapness to them and if you can afford to pull off this siding and restore the original wood siding beneath it, your house will be much more appealing. The HUGE downside of trying to restore the original siding is that it had likely been painted with lead based paint. With this being said, local codes will dictate that you may need to wrap or cover the entire house before sanding it, or remove the lead painted wood siding and start from scratch. I ran into this situation once when I was flipping a house. We pulled all of the aluminum siding off to expose the original wood siding. The wood siding needed a lot of work, but it was nice. We tested the paint and realized it was lead based paint. The neighbors were nervous about us sanding the siding near their house. We had two options: cover the entire exterior in tarps and refinish the siding or tear off the old siding and start fresh. We measured and weighed the cost to do both and the prices were similar for both. We decided to completely stripped the house of all its siding and resided with Hardie® plank and cedar shake. We hired a contractor to do the work and it was completely finished within a week as opposed to the time it would have taken to tarp off the house, scrape, sand, bondo, caulk, putty, prime and paint the old siding.

Hardie® Plank

Hardie® Plank is a terrific type of siding that looks exactly like wood siding, but is way more resilient to the elements. It is similar to masonite, however masonite siding deteriorates over time and requires painting, caulking and routine upkeep. Hardie® Plank (a brand name) is a similar looking product but is made of cement and therefore does not rot. Most new homes and new siding use this product because of its durability and ease of use.

Hardie® Panel

Hardie® panels are common on new contemporary architectural homes. These large Hardie® panels are usually combined with a combination of nice stained wood siding and metal. Hardie® panels have a very unique look to them and tent to not work too well on older homes.

Cedar Siding

Cedar siding is the most commonly used siding type in the United States. Cedar is used on fences and other exterior items because of its resilience to weather. It can be painted, stained or left bare to slowly. Cedar siding is the typical siding on a house that overlaps each board from the bottom to the top of the house.

Brick or stone

Both brick and stone provide an excellent siding option. They are virtually indestructible as well as attractive. They do not require the routine maintenance that other types of siding require. The biggest drawback is price, although in some areas of the country it is still very affordable.

Stucco

Traditional stucco is made with cement and offers a solid, lasting, moisture proof siding. It is seen a great deal in the Southern United States and tropical climates where the climate would require constant upkeep on other types of siding. Another reason is that the solid cement siding keeps houses cooler than traditional siding.

Cedar shakes

For those who love the look of cedar shakes, it is an excellent alternative to cedar siding as it requires less maintenance. When treated with stain it does not rot or peel. In fact, some people prefer the weathered look of cedar shakes most commonly seen on Cape Cod style homes.

Veneer & synthetic siding

Veneer is the fake brick or stone siding that you sometimes see on homes. You have to get close up to notice that it is fake. This sort of siding is not highly recommended as it does not give you the quality or longevity.

Asbestos

Asbestos is a very strong siding product that was popular in the 60's and 70's until they realized it was a dangerous material to work with. You won't be reinstalling this type of siding any time soon, but you may be repairing it if you purchase an old home. You can purchase a fiber cement replacement for asbestos that matches your siding whether it be the rectangular type or the wavy type. I have personally used this replacement material and it looks just like asbestos siding when you install and blend with the asbestos siding on your home.

Eaves

The exterior of a house containing eaves looks much better than a home without. An eave is the edge of a roof that the gutter is nailed into. In most cases, eaves project beyond the side of the building. Unfortunately, there are many homes, including brand new ones, where the eaves end just above the exterior wall of the house.

An example of an attractive eave would be on craftsman style homes. The eves extend several feet beyond the exterior wall of the house. Eaves are a feature you may not have given much attention too. You may see a house and love the appearance due to the appearance of the intricate exterior millwork and quality of the eves. In other cases, you may see a house that appears incomplete to you, or unflattering. These homes may barely have eves. I know this because I unfortunately own a house like this. A house without eves looks like a cheap box. When I see a house absent of eves, I immediately get the feeling that the builder or owner could not afford an entire roof, so they cut it off right at the exterior wall of the house. Eaves shade your windows, protect your walls from the sun, icicles, rain, snow, etc. Eaves are a beautiful part of a home and without them, homes can appear unfinished or unflattering.

One big reason that some homes don't have eaves is when builders in high density or urban neighborhoods are building to maximize interior square feet. Builders want the footprint of the house to be as large as possible. When this happens, the roof can not extend to far past the edge of the house or the house will encroach on the neighbors property and will not meet code requirements. So often times, you will see huge new homes with no eaves because the builder places more emphasis on interior square footage versus outdoor space or aesthetics.

The solution to no eaves:

If your home falls under the last example where the builder excluded eaves to maximize interior space, then chances are, you are already using all of the allowable space on your lot and will not be allowed to extend your eaves. However, if your home has plenty of space around it and you think the builder or original home owner was cutting costs by not extending the roof, then you do have options.

Adding eaves:

- You need to be sure that you have or can get the same roofing materials that are currently on your house, because when you add the eaves, you will need to have it shingled or roofed.

- Hire a framer/roofer to frame your eaves which will extend from the top of your exterior walls outward.
- The framer will have to top off the framing with plywood or roof sheeting to meet up perfectly with the existing roof sheeting.
- A layer of tar paper will be applied to the wood sheeting
- A roofer or framer will shingle the roof with the same materials to match the existing roofing.

Your new roof will be a gorgeous improvement to your home. If you can match the roofing materials, this entire project might not cost as much as you would expect. The expense definitely depends on the parameter of your roof.

In order to enhance the look of your eaves with a finished and flawless appearance, you can install soffits.

Soffits

Soffits are the underside of a construction element. In this case, soffits are the underside of eaves. Soffits are another classic touch you can put onto a house to give it a finished look. If your home already has soffits, perhaps you could clean them up with some crack filler and a fresh coat of paint. However, if you currently do not have soffits, you may want to strongly consider this addition to the exterior of your home.

The soffit extends from the side of the house to the edge of the eave and closes the space beneath the eave. Soffits can be constructed of many different materials and come in a variety of styles. The most common materials for soffits are tongue and groove wood. However, some houses have soffits made of aluminum and/or vinyl. The material used on your soffits will often coincide with the siding on your home. Some soffits are vented, while most are solid. Many people install recessed can lights in soffits for additional outdoor lighting or effect.

Having a well polished house will set your home apart from the neighbors. Soffits add a classic style and custom finish to any home.

Replace Cracked Window Panes

Cracked window panes are unsightly. Some of us live in a house with cracked single pane windows and don't even notice it because we have become so accustomed to it. While we may be used to them, home buyers may notice right away. Cracked windows are unsafe and can be dangerous. Whether you have single pane windows, double pane or leaded glass windows, be sure to check all of the windows in your home for cracks and get them repaired.

Single pane windows:

Single panes windows are fairly easy to fix. You can try to replace them yourself or hire a company to do it for you. If you do it yourself, you first have to remove the glazing on the outside of the window. The glazing is the caulk/putty around the border of the glass that holds with window pane in place. Sometimes it is too hard to remove and you need to take other measures. Since glazing will probably not come out easily, I take an additional step to protect myself against having a window shatter in my face. I get duct tape and tape a border around the window right on the glass. Then I stick lines of tape all the way across and diagonally. Then, while wearing gloves and eye protection, you can tap the glass with a hammer, lightly break it out and literally fold it up and throw away. Some stubborn broken pieces of glass will be stuck in the window frame with glazing. To remove these sections of broker glass, I rock the glass pieces back and forth which will loosen the glass from the window frame and allow you to steadily remove the glass. After you have all of the glass out of the window frame, use a scraper to scrape out the remaining glazing. Clean up your work space and be sure to get all the pieces of glass and fragments that may have gotten onto your floor with a shop vacuum. Measure the inside of the window frame for your new piece of glass. In most cases you can still go to a hardware store and have a piece of glass cut. If not, you may need to call a glass shop and have the piece custom cut for you. Along with your new piece of glass, you will need new glazing and small metal points. Bring home the glass, put it into the window frame, use the metal points to hold it into place and then glaze the window border. After the glazing dries, you can paint the glazing to match your window frame color.

Replacing a single pane window is something you can do yourself or hire someone to do if you are nervous about getting cut or not doing it right. If you have to hire someone to do it, the cost should still be quite low.

Double pane windows:

Replacing one of the window panes in a double pane window is not easy or recommended to be done by the homeowner. In this situation, I suggest that you call a couple different window places and get bids on either fixing the window pane or replacing the entire window all together.

Leaded glass windows:

Leaded glass windows are decorative windows made of small sections of glass supported by lead frames. Traditional lead windows are generally non-pictorial, as opposed to stained glass windows. Leaded windows contain geometric shapes and the glass sometimes contains beveled edges which reflected the light throughout a room in magnificent ways. Replacing broken panes of glass in leaded glass windows is not an easy task. There are companies that specialize in leaded glass window pane replacement. You can expect the cost to be around $150 per pane of glass, even if it is only 2 inches by 2 inch.

Replace Windows

Great windows give you double the satisfaction of most improvements because the improvement can be witnessed from both the interior and exterior of the home.

You have many choices when replacing your windows. You may be upgrading from old single pane metal windows to a nicer double pane wood window to match the architectural features of your house. Or maybe the old single pane wood windows are letting out too much heat in the winter so you have decided to upgrade to some more efficient double pan vinyl windows?

Regardless of the reasons, there is nothing like windows that are new, crystal clear, efficient and open and close with ease. New windows make a bright improvement to any home. A couple things to note when deciding which type of windows to purchase begins with the style of your home and your future plans. For example, you cannot paint vinyl windows. While vinyl windows come in many different colors, you may not want to be stuck with one color for the duration of your stay at the home. Many people choose wood windows because of the more classic rich look and because wood can be painted any color you choose (because wood is paintable you can change your mind over and over again about exterior paint colors). When choosing your new windows, you also have different choices of glass. You can choose single pane, double pane or triple pain windows which are both efficient and sound deadening. You can order glass that is UV protective for increased efficiency, but unfortunately they have a slight color differentiation.

To keep things simple, if you are upgrading your windows, I would recommend avoiding the UV protective windows because the color of the glass may clash with the house. Keep it simple; go with regular double pane windows in either vinyl or wood frames. Shop around because there is a lot of variation in price from company to company. You can expect a price range of $500 - $1000 per window if you hire a company to handle everything.

Add Window(s) for Light

Adding windows to a home is a larger project than most home owners will choose to take on. However, there may be a big opportunity to make a huge impression on potential buyers by adding some natural light to a room that doesn't already have windows or does not have enough windows.

The downside of adding windows to your home is the potentially high cost. You will need a knowledgeable contractor to cut a clean opening in an exterior wall of your home, carefully cutting through drywall, insulation, framing and siding. The opening will need to be precisely framed to fit the new window. The new window will have to be purchased (custom ordered if not a standard size) and must match the style and quality level of the existing windows. Then the window needs to be installed. After installed, the siding has to be repaired, drywall and both interior and exterior trim work and paint. Unless you are adding multiple windows, the expense of adding a single window may not increase the value of your home as much as the headache and cost to install one.

Install Shutter and Window Box Sets that Match

Shutters are not as common today and they used to be. Shutters are more of an East Coast aesthetic and most common in small rural towns. If shutters are popular home features in your neighborhood and your house seems misplaced without them, then by all means, install some shutters. Shutters add dimension and a classic touch to a home. Shutters offer another opportunity to add a color to your home. Even if the color is a basic white or black, it can be the additional color you needed to make your house stand out. Again, shutters are not common in all neighborhoods, so they may not pertain to your style of house or neighborhood. If shutters are common in your neighborhood and for some reason your home never had shutters or they are old and damaged, get a bid and explore the option of installing some. It could be the final touch on your house that persuades buyers to jump on your house over another.

Add Electrical Receptacles Outdoors

Adding electrical outlets to the exterior of your home will improve the value of your home because you will be adding a useful feature to the home. Unfortunately though, when buyers are previewing potential homes to purchase, they likely will not notice whether you have outdoor outlets or not. An inspector may notice that you do not have any outdoor outlets and call it out in the inspection report as an item that you need to add. You can refuse to add them, but it is just one more negotiating point that a buyer will have against you to try and get you to reduce your price mid-way through the sale.

Outdoor outlets are a necessity for holiday lighting, landscape lighting, outdoor fountains, electrical outdoor lawn equipment such as hedge trimmers, weed whackers, lawnmowers and any other outdoor electrical usage. Having outdoor outlets gives will not only present a more functional home for buyers, but it gives you more options for impressing potential buyers with outdoor features to increase curb appeal such as landscape lighting or a fountain.

The cost to add an outdoor electrical receptacle could be $250-$500 depending upon multiple factors. You will have to hire an electrician because you will be adding a circuit to your electrical panel, then running a line to the exterior of your house with the installation of an outdoor protective outlet box. You have the cost of the electrician's labor plus supplies.

Exterior/Outdoor Landscape Lighting

Outdoor lighting can be a fantastic improvement to your home. Whether you are adding uplighting to your house or trees, lights along a fence or a lighted walkway, lighting can add ambience, drama and security to your home at night.

Uplighting

Uplighting is common on high-end homes and often used to highlight landscape features such as trees, shrubs, hedges, fountains and other types of plant life. People also use uplighting to light up the exterior of their home. Uplighting is a great aesthetic to a home in the evening. Uplighting is not for every home and unless buyers are going to be previewing your home at night, it may not be a necessary expense to sell your home.

Fence lighting

Lights along a fence are not a popular feature but it creates I great custom look to a home and border for your property.

Lighted walkway

Probably the most common of exterior lighting is lighting along paths, walkways and stairs on the property. Walkway lighting serves as both a safety feature for guests at night while boosting curb appeal.

Exterior lighting can vary greatly in cost depending upon how you install it. If you want to add exterior lighting yourself at a reasonable cost, it can be done with little experience, skill or cost. Home improvement stores sell exterior home lighting kits. You can buy kits that have up lighting for your trees, house and hedges along with walkway lights. You stick the lights in the ground where you want them, then connect them with the wiring provided. The lights will plug into an exterior electrical socket. You can plug the lights in every night or put the lights on a timer so they come on for 3 - 4 hours every night at dusk and turn off by themselves. A kit for exterior lights to install yourself can cost from $150 - $400 depending upon the number of lights you get. A more expensive option is to hire an electrician or landscape architect to install high quality lights. The least expensive option for outdoor lighting is solar lighting. You can purchase solar lights to light up your pathway. Solar outdoor lights are inexpensive and there is no need for wiring. However, solar lighting has a bluish tint, are not very bright and does not last for more than a couple of hours.

In conclusion, if your property or house contains exterior features that would greatly benefit from some sort of lighting, you should definitely consider exterior lighting. And if your home is a high-end home, you should have professionals install the lighting. If you are on a budget, buy the kit yourself along with a timer for under $350 and create a home exterior that looks like you spent $3500.

Add Outdoor Faucets

Most houses already have at least one existing outdoor faucet. However, if you find that you also need a water faucet on the opposite side of the house to where your only faucet is located; this would be a great feature to consider adding. Adding an outdoor faucet can be an expensive endeavor if you have a finished basement and you need to run a water line from one side of the house to the other in order to accomplish this new faucet addition. If you need to open up drywall, do not waste your time with this improvement. However, if you find that adding an outdoor faucet can be done easily (you have an unfinished basement with exposed ceilings to run your water line), then this would definitely add value and function to your home for a reasonable cost.

Add Sprinkler System

An in-ground sprinkler system is a fantastic convenience element to add to your home that can save future home owners time and energy. An automated convenience such as an irrigation system that waters the entire yard and planting beds can add value to your home. There are a couple different installation options for in-ground irrigation systems just as there are with landscape lighting: You can hire an irrigation professional to install and service your irrigation system or purchase a consumer irrigation system and install it yourself.

Clearly it will cost more if you hire a professional. If you are selling a high end home to demanding buyers paying top dollar, then a professionally installed sprinkler system will be your best option. However, if you are in a moderately priced home and you feel as though buyers in your part of the country will appreciate and have a need for an irrigation system, then you can build one yourself using supplies from a local hardware or home improvement store. Available for install by homeowners, you can purchase both in ground and above ground sprinkler systems for a reasonable cost which can be put installed in a day. Once built, you can put the hose on a timer to run an hour per day.

Insulate All Exposed Pipes

Insulating exposed pipes is one of those maintenance items where an ounce of prevention is worth a pound of cure. The prevention is easy. Pro-active maintenance such as insulating exterior pipes will mitigate headaches in the future with bursting pipes or floods in the house due to water pipes freezing, expanding, bursting and flooding into the home.

Perform a thorough check of your home to see if you have exposed piping outside or in un-insulated spaces such as a crawlspace, attic or outside walls.

If you find exposed pipe, you should insulate them. The materials to insulate pipes are inexpensive and the job does not require a high level of skill. However, it does require patience and care to ensure that pipes are completely insulated.

There are a number of different options for insulating pipes. One option is to wrap pipes with regular fiberglass attic insulation (blanket and bat) around pipes. Another option, which is preferred and easier is the foam or fiberglass tubing (also called "tubular sleeve insulation") that is made specifically for pipes and sold at hardware stores.

Once you have determined which insulation you will use, begin by making sure you remove any dirt or grease from the pipe. Once the pipes have dried thoroughly you can begin wrapping them with insulation. Make sure you cover the pipe completely, taking extra care at corners wherever two sleeves or pieces of insulation meet. Wrap these areas with duct tape to seal them completely.

Once all of your pipes are completely wrapped with some sort of insulation and taped tightly, you may need to caulk around pipes where they enter your house from the outside.

Insulated pipes around your home are an attention to detail that a potential buyer with take note of.

Replace Rotted Wood (caused by dry rot or insects)

Dry rot is a weakening of wood caused by fungus. Dry rot is a result of too much moisture in contact with wood. The wood on your home most commonly affected by dry rot includes supporting posts, pillars, floor joists and beams beneath the house. Other areas on the house that can be damaged by dry rot included siding, beneath the siding, window trim and the roof (beneath the shingles).

Dry rot is an issue because the fungus eats away at the parts of the wood that give the wood strength and stiffness. The wood becomes dry and very weak. A trait of dry rot is that you can chip away at it with your fingers.

Another issue you can have with wood is wood destroying insects such as carpenter ants and termites. Dry rot is often confused with carpenter ant or termite damage. Carpenter ant damage is different in that insects actually remove wood by creating small holes and tunnels to live in. The removal of wood weakens the wood.

If it is evident that wood that supports your home has been destroyed by either dry rot or insects, you should consider having it replaced or treating the damaged areas before trying to sell your home. Dry rot and insect infested wood are two items that will most definitely be called out on an inspection report if seen and you will most likely be asked to replace it before the home sells. It is suggested to do your own home inspection to determine if you have dry rot or wood destroying insects prior to listing your home to avoid future pitfalls and setbacks when selling.

Replace Front Door

A unique front door will make a world of difference to the curb appeal of your home. It is hard to believe that something so simple which costs only $400 - $1,200 can make such a difference to your home. If you have a plain or unattractive front door that does nothing to benefit your house, take a trip to your local door store and look at all of the options. You can purchase a custom door and have it matched to replace your current door and hung by the same company. You may choose a door that has windows in it or a rustic style wood door with a peep hole that slides open and shut. The options are endless to meet your financial and design needs.

In addition to the improved look a new door can have on your house, a new door will keep out drafts and other weather related issues and therefore can save on your home's energy usage. The biggest benefit of changing your front door prior to selling your home is to improve the look of your home and make it stand out amongst the rest. Replacing a door solely for better efficiency would be more important if you intended on living in the house for a year or more. You main focus for selling should be whether the front door adds or detracts from the look and value of your home.

If you replace a door because you are seeking improved efficiency, you should understand the different types of doors that are available so you can make the best decision for your home. The following types of doors are available:

Wood

Solid wood doors are beautiful but the least energy-efficient. Temperature and humidity changes cause the door to swell and shrink. Wood doors also warp, bow and crack, making it almost impossible to get a weather-tight seal even with the best weather stripping. If you are buying a door to improve the look of your house, you will most likely buy a wood door because for the most part, they look the best and will not fail for over 10 years at least.

Fiberglass

Fiberglass doors are not very common, yet they rate the best on strength, durability, energy efficiency and its variety of style choices. The highest-quality versions of these doors look almost like real wood (if real wood was plastic and shiny…).

Insulated wood

Insulated wood doors offer the look of wood doors plus the efficiency of its insulation to better keep out the elements. These types of doors are wood veneer doors filled with a foam insulation core. Narrow strips of wood are installed along the edges to give the door a solid wood appearance.

Steel

A steel door is similar to an insulated wood door in that it also has foam insulation inside. The difference is that is has a steel outer coating which makes it more durable and energy efficient.

In addition to the different products used to make exterior doors, many different design styles are available to select from. As you search through the different style of doors for ones you like, be sure to stay true to the style of your house. The style of your home should limit the selection of doors you have to choose from. There are three basic door designs and under each door design there is a sub-category of styles to match your home.

The three basic types of door design are All Panel, Glass Panel, and Dutch. Each door type has multiple style categories under each offering a variety of styles to meet your needs depending on what type of home you are seeking a door for. The sub-categories under each door type are traditional, craftsman, contemporary and rustic. In addition to these categories, there are options for color and design, type and location of glass, and ornamentals on the door, etc.

Regardless of the material or style you choose, updating a door refreshes the look of your home both outside and inside and can give your home a dramatic facelift and improve curb appeal for a reasonable price.

Paint Front Door

A less expensive but effective alternative to replacing your front door is to refinish or paint the front door. You can go with a classic color like red or black. Some people go with a unique accent color. Whatever you decide, this is a very inexpensive way to make the front of your house pop for a fraction of the cost of replacing your door.

Add or Remove Screen Door: (It keeps out insects, but does it take away from curb appeal?)

A screen door can be great in certain parts of the country where insects are more prevalent. You can leave the front door open, letting the fresh air circulate through your home while the screen door keeps unwanted insects and pests outside. However, a screen door can also detract from the curb appeal of your home as it can hide a beautiful front door. If insects are a problem in the Summer, I advise you to keep the screen door on your home or have one installed. If insects are not an issue where you live, and you are wondering why you have a screen door in front of your front door, wonder no longer and remove it. The front of your home will look so much better with only your front door showing. Store the screen door in a garage or basement in case the future home owner wants to reinstall it.

Front Porch Flooring

Front porches are a coveted feature of most homes. Since the front porch is the entrance to the home it creates the first impression of the home and sets the standard for the remainder of the tour. You may not see the porch flooring from the street, but if a potential buyer intends on entering your home, they will ultimately end up on the front porch. Most front porch floors, if covered, are in decent shape. Take a look at your front porch floor and try viewing it from a third person point of view.

Is the wood in good shape?

If you have any rotted wood on your porch floor you should replace it. Be aware that sometimes you have to sacrifice a good floor board to remove the bad one. Don't worry about ruining a board as long as you have access to the same type of wood at the lumber store. After replacing the rotted wood, you may want to consider refinishing or repainting the floor so that the new and old boards match. Unlike a deck, you may not be able to pressure wash a front porch floor as it may be over a living space or finished area (the water would leak through the floor into your living space beneath). You may have to sand the floor to refinish it. Replacing rotted wood on your porch is something you may be able to do yourself with a saw, hammer, flat bar and tape measure. If not, obtain bids from several local handymen.

Is the paint chipping or worn away in the traffic areas?

If the paint is chipping, but the wood is in good shape, then this is a quick and easy fix. Remove all of the furniture from the porch, scrape the floor and repaint with floor grade paint (paint designed for high traffic areas). A fresh coat of floor paint on the floor of your porch will really liven up the entrance and create a better first impression for your guests.

Improve Porch Railings

Your front porch (if you have one) is a major part of curb appeal. It is the focal point of your home. If your porch railings are in bad shape, or cheap, then it cheapens the entire house. Look at your front porch and try to determine whether you are putting your best foot forward. The porch railings are visible from the streets, so this is even more important than the flooring.

A few ways you can improve your porch railings are by changing the look, repairing the railings and simply painting the railings.

Changing the look

There are lots of different types of porch and deck railings. Some will accent your house better than others. You have contemporary options and classic options to match craftsman homes and Victorian homes. If your home is older you may go for a more ornamental hand rail with vertical spindles. A contemporary railing may consist of a flat wooden top rail with horizontal cabling or thick glass panels in between the posts. There are a variety of different styles and materials that you can use for deck railing. If it is not too late, I would avoid the plastic railing material that is designed to look like old fashioned wood railings. Plastic railings and fences are very cheap and you can tell when you touch it. If you know a good carpenter, you can have a very nice railing system built to compliment your house perfectly, giving a superb first impression to all buyers that grace your home.

Repairing railings

If your railings already contain the original look of your home, but are falling apart, you may just need to rejuvenate them with the help of a handyman or carpenter. Most wooden parts of a railing system are common and you can find them at lumber yards and specialty wood stores to replace missing or broken parts of your railing. If you can salvage the nice railing you have, you should do it and stay with the original look of the house, unless the original look was a cheap thrown together railing built by someone with no money or taste.

Repaint

Many railings are in decent shape and just need to be cleaned up, scraped, maybe sanded, primed and painted. It is amazing what a coat of paint can do to liven up the railings on your deck. I recently had the railings on the front porch of one of my rental properties painted bright white. Every time I drive by this house I am taken back by how much better the entire house looks just because of these two railings that I had painted white. It makes a huge difference.

I said it before and I will say it many more times: Curb Appeal is so important for making that first impression.

Install Solar Energy Panels

Solar panels will increase the value of both new and old homes. The value of solar energy panels installed on a home will appreciate over time as the cost of electricity increases. Best of all, a solar home will sell twice as fast as a home without solar panels according to the U.S. Department of Energy Efficiency & Renewable Energy.

The trend for eco-friendly and green homes is swelling with intensity lately. It was common knowledge for all of us that investing most of our money into a kitchen remodel would result in the largest return on investment. Lately, things are starting to shift a bit and features such as solar panels to replace a home's need for electricity is rising in importance. Renewable energy commands a higher purchase price from buyers. As I mentioned earlier, a green certified home can sell for up to 9% more than a standard home.

Solar energy does not only reduce your electric bill, it can also reduce your gas bill if you replace some of the gas appliances with electric ones. However, since appliances that use gas in your home use so much energy, you may not have enough solar power to run these appliances for a full day. Therefore, it is best to only use solar power for existing items in your home which are currently electric such as the refrigerator, the lights, the computer, the TV, stereo equipment, motors in the electric furnace, ceiling fans, washing machine, etc.

The demand for a remodeled kitchen will be higher in some areas, while the demand for solar energy may be more popular in others. Know your target audience and do what will net you the most value in your particular housing market.

Street Numbers

Buyers notice when a home owner appears to take care of their property. If an owner pays attention to small details, then there is a good chance, the house will be in tip top shape. A little detail like having the house numbers freshly painted (Stenciled) onto your street curb will make a good impression on potential buyers. It tells a buyer that you are a meticulous home owner and pay attention to details when caring for a home.

New Mailbox

Replacing the mailbox with a brand new mailbox is not going to make a huge difference in the value of your home. However a new mailbox will complete the polished look of your wonderful home as potential buyers approach your driveway and front door. The first impression of your home is paramount and the mailbox is typically the first element of your home that people see.

Mailboxes come in a variety of shapes and sizes. You can get away with the standard silver, black or white metal mailbox. Or if you want to step it up a notch, they make mailboxes that look like small cedar homes. Beyond that, the options are endless, but there is no reason to go beyond this point because ultimately the mailbox will not sell your home. I just want to reiterate that it is the first impression people will have when they see your home and it is better to put your best foot forward and replace that old rusty and dented mailbox that you have gotten so used to reaching your hand into daily to grab your big electric and gas bills because you don't have solar panels yet.

House Numbers

Everyone has house numbers. If you don't have a concrete road in front of your house and the ability to paint new numbers on the curb, then you can replace your address numbers on the house. Home improvement stores have a large variety of house numbers. You can go with large wood numbers or stainless steel, brushed nickel, brass, etc. There are many ways to display your house numbers. Most people already have house numbers so you are just replacing with similar new numbers to brighten up the look of your home from the street. My favorite house numbers if you prefer the contemporary look are the raised brushed metal house numbers. The numbers look like they are floating an inch away from your house and are really sharp. You can buy them at most home improvement stores.

Power Wash the Exterior of Your Home

If you have any sort of brickwork or concrete on the exterior of your home, walkway or patio, you will want to seriously consider cleaning it up. You will be amazed at how dirty your concrete is once you start pressure washing away the black and green dirt and mold that has accumulated on it. Rent a pressure washer from your local home improvement store and pressure wash the sidewalks and walkways to your front door. If your front porch steps and porch floor are concrete, pressurewash them too. Some houses have retaining walls or brickwork at the base of the house or somewhere along the front. If this is the case, then pressure washing them will brighten up these areas and make them look virtually new again.

I would not recommend using any type of soap. The pressure of the water will do the trick on its own and you don't want to pollute the environment with soap.

Here are some useful tips to know about when pressure washing:

- You need good water pressure from the water source you are going to use. If your outdoor water faucet has poor water pressure, offer your neighbor some money to use their water faucet.

- If you rent or purchase a pressure washer, there are two key things to take note of: The Pressure per square inch (PSI) and the Gallons per minute (GPM). When spraying concrete you want the PSI to be at least 1500 and your GPM should be at least 4. Many of the cheap pressure washers (purchase price below $800) have low GPM and it is not enough pressure to clean anything. A nice high GPM means a lot of water is coming out at a high speed and it will clean everything exactly as it should. Be careful not to clean your toes off.

- A 25-45 degree tip should do the trick. Do not use the 0 degree tip unless you intend to sign your name in the concrete.

Pressure washing your home is an inexpensive do-it-yourself way to instantly improve the look of your home. Add this very important improvement to your list if you have concrete elements to your exterior.

Upgrade Drainage System: Sewer line

Make sure your sewer line is in tip top shape. If you know your sewer line is not in good shape, then don't bother trying to sell the house without first fixing it because an inspector will discover the issue and it will hold up the closing of your home until you repair it or reduce your sales price to compensate the buyer.

How can you tell if your sewer line is in need of repair? Your sewer line can either become blocked or clogged. I have illustrated below some ways to determine whether your sewer line is broken or clogged. There are a few ways to determine on your own what is wrong before calling a professional and spending hundreds of dollars.

The first thing to do is to call the city maintenance department and find out if there was a sewer line back up in the neighborhood. If there is a sewer line problem nearby, you can save yourself a lot of time and worry because it is the city's issue and not yours (unless it backs up into your home).

If you are connected to the city sewer line, here are some ways to tell if you have a broken sewer line:

If you have determined that the city is not at fault for your sewer line issue, exam your property where the sewer line runs from your house and connects to the city's sewer pipe. Of course, you will not actually see the pipe because it is below the surface, but if you know the general area of the pipe, you can follow it for examination of the soil. If you see a puddle of water and it hasn't rained in a while, you probably have a broken sewer pipe. If you don't see any standing water, look even harder and see if you notice any soft or mushy spots in the yard. Lastly, do you notice a dirty odor along around the vicinity of your yard where the sewer line runs? If you answered yes to any of these three issues, then there is a high probability that you have a broken sewer line between your house and where your sewer line connects with the city. At least now when you call a plumber you can save some money by pinpointing the area of concern.

Signs that you have a clogged Sewer Line

After you have called the city and learned that there is not a city sewer line issue, and you have tried all of the above checks for a broken sewer line, try the following ideas to check if your sewer line is clogged. Flush your toilet and examine the water level as the bowl fills back up. The water bowl should fill back up to its original location. If it does not, this could be an indication that your pipe is blocked. Another way to check for blockage is to examine the drains in your home. If the water does not drain or if the water is coming back up into your shower or tub drains, this indicates a clogged sewer pipe. Another great way to tell if your pipes are clogged is to listen to the pipes as the water drains. When pipes are clogged, you will witness gurgling noises in your drains. In the same situation, you may have bubbles coming up in your toilet. Lastly, you may be able to identify a root problem in your yard. Take a look outside along the path of your sewer line to see if you have trees, shrubs or large plant life that may be encroaching upon your underground pipes. There is a very good chance that a small tree has roots invading your pipes. A plumber with a sewer camera will be able to tell you if you have roots and if so, he/she can help locate which tree or plant the roots are coming from.

Once you have determined that your sewer line is either broken or clogged, you need to call a professional to repair it. If the sewer line is merely clogged, a plumbing professional should be able to root out the drain and clear a pathway for less than $500.00 including all of the camera work to identify the problem. However, if your sewer line is broken, you have a much larger problem and will need to have pipe replaced. Generally the pipe is over 4 feet below the ground. Depending upon the topography of your yard and location of the break, replacing a broken sewer line can start at $2000 and cost upwards of $10,000 - $12,000 to fix.

If your sewer line does not connect to the city sewer system, then you may have an issue with your septic system. Hire a professional to help you examine your septic system. If the septic system needs to be replaced, it generally costs over $10,000 to replace.

A bad sewer line or septic system will be exposed during the buyer's inspection on your home. Make sure your sewer system is operating properly before putting your home on the market to avoid pitfalls and setbacks during the sale.

Test and/or Repair All Outdoor Drains to Prevent Flooding (Your standard homeowner's insurance policy will not protect you from flooding in your home caused by outside water coming in.)

Before you list your home for sale, do this very important examination that can potentially save you thousands of dollars. Be sure all exterior drainage around your property is functioning properly. Different types of exterior drains to examine are: Driveway drains, floors drains at exterior basement doors and downspout drains.

Driveway drains

If you have a drain in your driveway, it was installed for a reason. The drain is intended to keep water out of your garage or living areas. The problem with outdoor drains is that they get more debris in them than interior drains because they are exposed to tree debris, dirt, leaves and pine needles. Once enough pine needles and debris get into your exterior drain, the drain will no longer work and water will build up around the drain during a rain storm, eventually flooding its surroundings. Flooding your garage can be an issue if you are storing personal belongings or furniture on the floor. In addition to protecting your own personal belongings, you don't want a potential buyer to pull up to your home and see standing water. One good way to prevent this is to run water into the drain with a hose and check the flow. If the flow is a little slow or backed up, you may be able to remedy the clog by purchasing and using a rubber drain bladder. A drain bladder is an oval shaped rubber tube that connects to the end of a hose. After purchasing the right size bladder for your drain, you stick the bladder into the drain hole, then turn on the hose to blast the drain line with water. The pressure will build up in the bladder and the water shoots out into the drain like a small pressure washer and can eliminate blockage and force the debris and water down the drain. If this does not work, you will need a professional to root out the drain for you.

Exterior basement door drains

These are the small drains in the center of the cement pad at your basement or backdoor. This is one of the most important drains on your property because its failure can cause thousands of dollars of damage. Unlike a driveway drain which may leak into your garage and damage a couple of boxes, when this particular drain clogs, you flood finished living space. Living space may contact carpeting, furniture, drywall, millwork (trim) and insulation. If any of these items become wet from outside water, it is considered contaminated and must be replaced. These drains, being small, will easily clog with dirt, sand and debris causing major damage to your home. You know what is even worse? Most home insurance policies will not cover flooding from water that enters your home from the outside. This means that you are on the hook for 100% of the damages to your home even if you have home owners insurance. Use the drain bladder to remove the clog or hire a professional for assistance.

I completely remodeled a home to sell it. We spent a lot of money finishing the basement to increase the livable area. While the house was on the market, we had a big rain storm. The drain failed at the back basement door and flooded our new carpeting in the basement. Because we re-landscaped the exterior, there was more debris in the drain than we had realized and it blocked up during a storm. Learn from my mistake!

Downspout drains

If your downspouts connect directly to drain pipes in the ground alongside your home, then you will want to be sure these storm water drains are clear. If you live near trees, your gutter could send a lot of debris down your downspouts causing clogs in your downspouts and drains. Next time it rains, walk the parameter of your home and make sure there is no water overflowing out of these drains. If so, you will need to pull the downspout out of the drain and clear the drain out. You can do this with a larger drain bladder. My only caution is that if your storm water drain pipes are old concrete or clay pipes, you need to be careful because the bladder can actually crack the frail pipes when it expands. You may want to consult a professional to unclog old storm drain pipes.

Make Your Home Flood Proof with an Exterior or Interior French Drain and Sump Pump

Is your home prone to flooding in wet weather? Living space that floods is hardly considered living space because nobody will want to put anything of value in a space that has the potential to flood. If flooding has been an issue, you can improve the marketability of your home if you can install a permanent fix such as an exterior or interior French drain. If you can show that you installed proper drainage to prevent your home from flooding ever again your buyers' pocket books will begin to loosen up. With a finished basement that includes carpeting or hardwood floors, you cannot take any chances of your home flooding. There are multiple remedies for flooding, but I am going to mention the two best ones in my opinion.

Before you spend a lot of money digging down along your foundation and waterproofing it or installing drains around your home there may be a simple fix. In many instances, water in the basement is a result of poorly functioning or installed downspouts. Sometimes it can be a missing downspout or the downspout is not properly directing the water away from the house. I mention this elsewhere in the book. The first thing you should do when you notice any water coming into the house is to determine where the water is coming, then go outside to that area and see if your gutters are leaking or if your downspout is dropping the water right in the general area where the leak is coming into the house. If so, your fix is simple: re-route the downspout so the water flows away from the house. Test this out over the next couple of rainstorms and see if the downspout was the culprit.

If you were not lucky enough to find a faulty downspout then you have a bigger problem of ground water enter your home. To guarantee no more water comes into the house you can either have professional install a French drain around the exterior parameter of your house or you can have a French drain installed on the inside of your home along the exterior wall parameter of your house. The reason I suggest hiring a professional is because their work is typically guaranteed and if something goes wrong, you can contact them to fix it. You can install French drains yourself, but it is time consuming, back breaking work with no guarantees that it will work properly.

Exterior french drain

First off, a French drain is a trench that is dug and filled with fabric, perforated PVC pipe covered in gravel or crushed rock then covered with soil. The purpose of a French drain is to reroute water from one area to another location. In this instance, I am talking about a drain that runs the parameter of your home, captures water and moves it away from the house. The collected water follows the drain as it slopes downward and eventually into a storm drain, ditch or some sort of drain field underground that you have installed. French drains are the most common fix for flooding in basements. The cost is not as extraordinary as one would expect. I have seen them installed by professionals for as low at $1,000. You are paying mostly for labor and it can be done within a day or two.

Interior French Drain

The interior French drain is the same exact concept as the exterior French drain except the French drain is installed from inside the house beneath the floor and guaranteed to catch all of the storm water before it enters the house. I have watched the professionals install interior French drains in a very nice finished basement and it was less invasive than I would have expected. The professionals pulled back the carpet and exposed the concrete along all exterior walls of the basement. They removed trim and even some tile in a bathroom along the exterior wall. In one day the contractors jack-hammered a 6 inch wide trough along the entire parameter of the basement exposing the dirt. Believe it or not, a jack hammer does not make a huge mess or kick up a lot of dust like a concrete saw. The professionals dug some dirt out, installed the French drain, covered it back up with concrete and by day two it was complete. All that had to be done was for the tile to be put back, carpet and trim. The work was guaranteed and there was not digging outside. The gentleman who installed the drain were able to tie it into the storm drain outside without digging a giant hole and create a drain field in the yard which kept expenses down.

If you can show a potential buyer a receipt along with a warranty guaranteeing that the basement will have no flooding issues, it will put their mind at ease and make for an easier sale.

Add Exterior Trim

Some houses were built without exterior window trim. Typically these were homes built on a budget. Many times when you see homes or apartment buildings with old metal windows there is no exterior window trim. The siding buts right up the edges of the windows. Unless you have a mid-century modern house with floor to ceiling windows, a modern house or a contemporary home with a completely sophisticated look, a home without exterior window trim can appear unsightly and unfinished. In most cases, if your siding is wood, some sort of composite or even asbestos, a professional can easily remedy the situation and install exterior trim around the windows.

First you need to determine the type of trim you want around your windows. How wide or thick do you want your trim? What style of wood trim do you want? The simplest trim is a pre-primed wood trim that you can get at home improvement stores and lumber yards. It is typically a rough wood that you can get in 2-6 inch widths to wrap around the windows. The most basic exterior window trim would be a 4 to 6 in wide pre-primed wood that follows the parameter of the window. Another option, if you want to step up the quality of the trim around your windows, is to purchase better quality, decorative trim (unfinished or primed wood) to wrap your windows. Note that if you choose a window trim that is not perfectly flat or square, the installation becomes trickier because the cuts you make at the corners of your wood have to be precise so they perfectly match up at all corners. I would recommend hiring a carpenter if you choose a decorative trim style.

The next step, after you have determined the type and style of trim you are going to use is to cut a border around the window where you will install the new trim. Typically the trim does not go above the siding. Anytime you see exterior trim nailed on top of siding, it is a sign of an amateur carpenter. You need to cut away the siding so your new window trim is flush with the siding and the window. Cutting the trim away can be quite easy. Now that you know your trim width, you can draw (or snap) a line on the siding (all four sides) where you need to cut away the siding. Using a skill saw (I prefer a battery powered one), set the blade to a shallow depth so you only cut away the siding, then begin cutting away the siding on all four sides of the window. The 4-6 inch wide pieces of siding you want to remove should easily pull out.

If the tar paper is still intact, you shouldn't have to do much more prep work. However, you will need to place flashing along the top of all the windows you are trimming. Flashing is always installed along the top of your windows before you install your top piece of trim to the window. Flashing is a thin piece of metal that you can buy in strips at your local home improvement or hardware store. It is pre-shaped to sit right on top of your window and route water outward away from your house and window as rainwater approaches from above. This is a very easy piece to install and is an imperative step of the process.

Finally, using a nail gun, nails or screws, install the trim around the window. Use paintable exterior siding/trim caulk to fill any visible gaps in the trim work in addition to gaps between the window and trim and siding and trim.

Your window trim is complete and can be painted any color you wish to match your home and windows.

Exterior window trim is not for every home. However, it can do wonders for the curb appeal of an otherwise basic home that never had the element of exterior trim. Installing window trim is a fairly inexpensive task whether you take on the project yourself or hire someone for a day's work.

Full Green Lawn: Sod, Seed or Weed?

Have you lost the battle against weeds and moss in your yard? Or perhaps your lawn has been destroyed by dogs or other types of animals. When it comes time to sell, you might be surprised how inexpensive it is to re-sod your lawn. You have some different options which can affect your price. Just like many of the other improvement ideas in this book, you can do this project yourself to minimize cost or hire a professional to have it done quickly for a bit more money. The difference in cost from hiring someone versus doing this yourself is not that large, but the toll on your lower back could be great after all of the hauling, digging and excavating.

Option 1: The Pros

You can hire a professional company to tear off the top layer of grass and dirt. They will level the dirt and lay down brand new sod. You can have a brand new lawn in 1 to 2 days.

Option 2: Do-It-Yourself like the Pros

You can rent the same machine that the professionals use which slices the top layer of grass weeds and dirt to remove the existing lawn. The downside is that this can be cumbersome and you ultimately have to bend over and pick up all of the grass weeds and dirt you are throwing away and haul it to a yard waste or compost dump. If you don't have a truck already, you will have to rent one. You can use the same truck to purchase and pick up the perfect amount of Sod that you need to cover your yard (measure your square feet and purchase the amount that matches plus a little extra), or hire the local home improvement store to deliver the sod to your home. Laying out the sod is the easy part.

Option 3: Re-seed and save

Perform an extensive weed or moss killing campaign. Then if your lawn is still alive after all of the chemicals you just used to kill the weeds, you can rake some fresh dirt over parts of the lawn that need the most help, spread grass seed and water daily to thicken up the lawn with some fresh grass.

Whichever way you choose, your curb appeal will increase dramatically with a new lawn thick lawn. Even the third option above will make a dramatic difference if you have a couple of months to grow a new lawn before you list the home.

Keep Lawn Well Mowed

If lack of grass is not a problem you have which requires sod, seeds or weeding, then you may be battling a completely different issue with tall out of control grass. Keeping your lawn mowed routinely around the time of your sale is one of the simplest and easiest of improvements. Before you even think about listing your home and definitely before you take photos or allow anyone to see the house, be sure your lawn is mowed. A height of 2 to 3 inches will give a nice uniform and well manicured appearance. Be careful as you cut. If you cut the lawn too short you will have yellow spots or circular mower blade marks. The professionals usually set their blades around 2 to 3 inches tall so you have a nice green lawn. Do not leave large clumps of cut grass on the lawn. Have it hauled away or composted. Fertilize and water as needed so when you mow it is still nice, green and plush. Keeping your law mowed will give your home a well maintained and polished look that will maximize curb appeal.

Fence

A fence can be the cause of a major increase in the value of your home. Especially if the fence increases needed privacy, compliments the look and feel of your home and improves curb appeal. A fence has to have at least one of these characteristics and if adding a fence hits 2 or 3 of these benefits at the same time, your return on investment will easily be greater than your cost and the improvement to your home will be substantial.

Aside from marking a property boundary or keeping a dog within property lines, most people install a fence for privacy. The common height restriction is 6 feet for a fence. Common fence materials are cedar plank. Fences can be purchase in 6 foot segments from large home improvement stores and installed by the home owner. Purchasing the fence in 6 foot segments would be the least expensive way to build a fence aside from building one from scratch. There are a variety of different fence styles and design. Many fence ideas you can pick up just by driving around the neighborhood.

The fence should complement the look and feel of your home. Take clues from other homes in the neighborhood and see what works and what doesn't.

Lastly, will the fence look good from the street? A white picket fence can be pretty nice. However, there are some really great fence ideas that are contemporary and sleek looking such as horizontal cedar or ironwood fences. A fence can cost $1,000 - $10,000 depending on materials and the length of your fence. Price it out with multiple contractors and materials to see what works for you. But don't build a cheap fence because the wrong fence could have a negative effect on your home value as opposed to a positive one. Stay away from chain link or plastic fences.

Repaint Fence and Trellis

If you already have fencing or a trellis, then simply repainting or refinishing a fence or trellis will make a dramatic improvement to your curb appeal. Paint fades quickly on fences as they weather in the rain, wind and sun. In dry climates the paint fades and in wetter climates fences turn green with mold. Many fences are close to plant life which will also create the perfect environment for mold and fungus buildup. Brighten up that fence with a fresh coat of paint. If you really want the paint to stick, it is best to clean the wood first. The most effective way to clean the wood (as long as you are careful and don't damage the old wood) is to pressure wash the fence or trellis. While cleaning the fence, trellis or outdoor wood work, it is a great time to replace or fix any loose or broken pieces of wood.

Depending on the weather, let the wood dry for a day or so if you pressure washed it and then paint. You may be able to use a roller to roll the paint on or rent a paint sprayer and tarp everything off really well so you don't paint your landscaping, neighbor's house or automobile.

The end result will be nice clean borders around your home with new looking wood work and greater curb appeal.

Outdoor Water Feature

Water Features are a terrific way to add value to your home while creating a destination point for your outdoor entertainment and personal relaxation. A well considered and implemented water feature can improve your property value as well. Stone waterfalls and ponds are used to create a magnificent backdrop and obscure or hide unsightly limitations in your yard. Bringing water into your backyard can create a soothing sound barrier when ambient noise in your neighborhood is a detraction from enjoying your home. Ponds and fountains attract wildlife and bring the seasons into focus throughout the garden year. A fountain or water feature near the back or front door creates a calming effect as you enter or exit your home each day.

Fountains and water features can be purchased at home improvement stores and nurseries. The price of fountains ranges from $100 for inexpensive plastic ones to over $1500 for beautiful multi-tiered stone fountains. The options for fountains are endless. There are fountains for every price point. You can even purchase fountains at home improvements stores that are made of plastic but mimic stone.

Other water features such as stone waterfalls and ponds are slightly more advanced. While stone waterfalls and ponds can be created by a homeowner, it is recommended that such a feature be left to a professional so that it looks right and operates properly. The costs vary greatly for this so you will have to get estimates to determine which is the best avenue for you.

Install Stone Patio

A stone patio is a great way to increase the value of your home and impress potential buyers. Home owners are attracted to the idea of having a nice spot outdoors to host parties in the spring and summer months in addition to having a comfortable place to cook outdoors.

Stone patios can be constructed of many different types of stone. Patios are either made of natural stone or manmade stone called pavers.

Natural stones:

Some of the different types of natural stone used for patios are slate, bluestone and fieldstone to name a few. Each type of stone can create a different look for your stone patio. Bluestone has a beautiful almost gray blue color to it making it one of the more popular stones that can be used to create a stone patio.

The benefits of a natural stone patio:

- The ability for the ground to still absorb water (earth friendly).
- You have the ability to add flowering ground cover to the patio in between the different size stones.
- Some people like natural stone patios because a natural stone patio has stones that are different shapes, sizes and thicknesses, giving each patio a unique look.

Manmade stones (Patio Pavers):

A paver is a generic term given to describe any regular type of brick that is specifically used for the construction of an outdoor patio deck. There are 3 common types of materials that are used for manufacturing paver products that can be used as patio pavers: Concrete, clay, sandstone and granite.

Each of the four paver types has a variety of different products that are manufactured in an endless selection of colors, shapes, sizes and patterns that are used in patio paving applications. Pavers are typically installed close together like a tile floor creating a nice clean look as opposed to natural stone patios which have plant life growing in between the stones, concrete or sand.

After you decide which type of stone you want to install, a natural stone patio or pavers, you will need to decide if this is a project that you are going to take on yourself or hire someone to do. The challenge in any outdoor patio besides the hard work involved and expense incurred buying materials is creating a perfect level finished surface. A stone patio with an uneven surface will be a nuisance on many levels beginning with the placement of the gas grill and lawn furniture, to issues with water flow and of course the dangers of loose footing for your guests.

An outdoor stone patio is proven to increase the value of homes. Buyers are sure to fall in love with the exterior before even entering the house when they see the beautiful stone patio. Because of the increased value of your home, you should be able to easily recoup the cost of installing the stone patio when you sell your home.

Create Privacy:

Privacy is a common motif under multiple topics such as fences and landscaping. However, for some of you, privacy may be an imperative improvement worthy of standing on its own. In high density/urban areas, your neighbors can be extremely close and finding privacy in your own yard can be scarce. In even worse situations, some homes are located close to apartment buildings or condominium complex where even a 6 foot fence will not give you enough privacy because the building nearby several stories tall.

Buyers value privacy and understand that in high density neighborhoods it is a rare commodity. If you can somehow create privacy from the neighbors in an area, just imagine how desirable your home will be as opposed to others who have a public back or front yard.

Privacy can be created in a number of ways. The two biggest and easiest ways are fences and trees. Most ordinances limit your fence height to 6 feet tall. If that is not enough, I have seen people use lattice to go higher for a little more privacy, but that could be construed as a fence.

Using trees as privacy is not a quick fix unless you can afford to buy and have professionally installed mature trees. There are multiple variations of trees that you can purchase in all different sizes. I found that most people choose evergreens so they have year-round privacy. In addition, varieties of evergreens grow very quickly giving you privacy within a few years. I cannot mention any specific tree breeds because the tree varieties people plant for privacy differ from state to state depending upon where you live and your climate. It is very possible to purchase trees that are 10 feet tall and have them planted. Within one week you can have complete privacy. Combine trees with a fence and you have yourself a private patio or mini-park in your back yard. I want to reiterate that if your home is in a high density area, spending some money to create a private outdoor area where outdoor privacy is scarce may boost your asking price considerably over the competition because your home with have a rare commodity than others do not possess.

Create a Rock Garden

Make your landscape maintenance free by creating a rock garden. A rock garden is a great way to add unique texture and color to your landscape. It is a less common approach to landscaping, but as you learn more about it online, in books and magazines, you will see how a rock garden can add a contemporary characteristic to your property boosting the over appeal of your home.

A rock garden can be made with mix large rocks, small shiny tones, multi-colored rocks or gravel. Upon the rocks you can strategically place pots and plants for added dimension.

Rock gardens can be created on flat surfaces or built into a sloping yard. Some people will only accent a garden with large rocks, others will have a rock garden full of different sized rocks combined with a water feature. Water features are an ideal focal point in a rock garden. They enhance the naturalistic feel and add another element of interest. Large rocks will have to be professionally delivered. Otherwise, you can pick up bags of stone and rock at your local home improvement store or stone stores.

Add a Hot Tub

If installed by professionals and with proper planning, a hot tub can make a great addition to a home.

Buying a used hot tub and putting it in a random spot in the backyard will most likely detract from your home value versus increase it. However, when done well, a hot tub can be a great selling feature of your home. An example of this being done correctly would be a small deck addition off the back of the house or enclosed area custom designed to fit the hot tub into. Hot tubs need a walkway so people don't track dirt or grass into the tub and they also need privacy from neighbors. If you can manage to combine both of these features, then you should be able to create an inviting hot tub that a buyer can envision themselves enjoying. I have seen hot tubs both enclosed and completely outdoors. Enclosed hot tubs are nice, but more troublesome because the steam will wreak havoc on your windows and your interior causing mold and mildew if not properly ventilated. The last important note to mention about installing a hot tub is choosing the right hot tub. Keep it simple. It is tempting to get the hot tub that seats 10 with the multi-colored lights and stereo system, but all people really want is a nice clean classic hot tub that seats 4-6 people.

Real estate professionals will argue for and against the installation of a hot tubs in regards to whether a hot tub improves your property value or not. The reason this goes both ways is because we have all seen Jacuzzi tubs that look good and others that are so bad you wouldn't get anywhere near them. So the fact of the matter is, a tub has to be installed nicely, in a location that easily accessible and stylistically attractive to the home and yard.

The ultimate point is that a hot tub can both improve and decrease the value of your home. Whether you already have a Jacuzzi / hot tub or are weighing the options of creating an oasis in your backyard, please consider all of your options to be sure you can deliver the spa-like retreat you are trying to create.

Add Lap Pool or Swimming Pool

Adding a lap pool or swimming pool can be a huge improvement to your home. However, let's be clear that we are not talking about an above ground pool you can buy from the large discount store. If you professionally install a pool with a surrounding concrete patio, you will have a hot commodity and be commanding an entirely new client base with more money. Keep in mind you will also scare away some people that do not want to be bothered with the expense and upkeep of a swimming pool. The value of this improvement will depend upon where you live too. If you get little sun per year, then a swimming pool is not necessary may actually deter some buyers. However, if you live in a mostly warm climate, then a pool is a necessity. Get bids from multiple vendors to build a swimming pool. You will also need room for the filtering equipment that goes along with the pool. This is an expensive improvement, but under the right circumstances, this could be the selling point of your home.

Remove Unwanted Trees and Shrubs

Remove the clutter from your yard and improve your curb appeal. If you have too many trees, don't be afraid to remove some by either chopping them down or digging them out and giving them away to someone who wants them (you would be surprised how many people will come dig a tree out of your yard so they can have a full grown mature tree for their yard. You can advertise the trees on craigslist under free stuff). Shrubs, bushes and trees can be beautiful but they can also be a hindrance over time. If not properly maintained, tree limbs mix with other tree branches and bushes creating quite a mess. If you are unclear about what exactly needs to be done with your trees, get some advice from some different for assistance before doing an irreversible damage. Don't be afraid to remove some large plant life if it means less clutter and making your home more visible from all sides. Your house will look much bigger when it is not hidden behind trees and bushes.

Landscaping Clean Up

Almost as important as painting the exterior of your home is the appearance of your landscape. Even if you don't have a professionally landscaped yard, it is still important to be sure your trees are property maintained and trimmed. Shrubs and bushes should be trimmed and tidy. Gardens and planting beds should be free of weeds and dead foliage removed. Use a dark mulch or beauty bark around trees and amongst planting beds to give your yard a polished look.

In addition to the dramatic improvement a tidy landscape and create, there are some other items you should be aware of with regards to the vegetation on your property. You do not want any of your bushes, shrubs, plants or trees touching the siding, windows, gutters or the roof of your house. There are multiple reasons why plant life should not touch your home. The first reason is that insects travel on plant life and will use plants and trees as a bridge to get onto your house, into the siding and into your home. The second reason is that when the wind blows or you have a steady daily breeze, vegetation will brush back and forth on your home and slowly damage whatever is in its path: siding or roof. A third reason is direct damage to your home due to growth. Trees and plant life can grow right through the roof of your house. Vines can grow beneath your siding and pull it away from the house and even remove gutters. The last reason is different types of rot on your home. Having vegetation resting on your wood siding or roof causes rotting of wood and roofing materials.

A good inspector will note the vegetation and plant life touching your home during an inspection and you may end up cutting back vegetation and trimming trees before your home will close. There are multiple reasons to properly trim back and landscape your property as noted above. Be one step ahead and make this improvement to protect the home while making your property look dramatically better.

Lawn

Keep the lawn mowed, trimmed and edged. Edging the yard, along the drive, around planting beds, along the sidewalk makes a world of difference. Add some plants where needed and your home will look great framed in by your beautiful yard.

Walkways

Walkways add curb appeal and charm to your home. Walkways can be made of many different surfaces and products. Some ideas for materials include pavers, concrete, brick, stone and the list goes on. Large home improvement stores will typically carry these various products for you to choose from for creating the perfect patios and walkways.

Walkway pavers are the most popular material to create nice smooth walkways. Pavers are typically placed tightly together so your walkway will not be riddled with weeds and grass. Poured concrete is nice for certain types of homes, but may lack style if you are intending to add some charm to your property. The other popular walkway style is the placement of various sized granite or slate pieces. The stone can be expensive at over $10 per piece, but has a natural feel that goes well with certain types of homes. Using large stones like this can create a beautiful walkway, but it can be bumpy and contain lots of weeds and grass if not maintained properly.

If you do not already have a walk way to your front door or to an outbuilding, then choosing the location for your walkway is easy. The best place to install walkways is where people have worn a track in your lawn. Installing a walkway where you have worn out the grass will improve your property in two ways: You can get rid of the unsightly dead grass / dirt walkway that was created from high traffic while adding a functional landscape feature bettering your curb appeal.

It doesn't matter what the situation is, walkway pavers will absolutely & completely change the atmosphere of your garden, paths, walkways. A nicely appointed walkway or path will add beauty & elegance to your landscape, making it much more user friendly & appealing. Walkways will increase the value of your home while completely changing the atmosphere of your yard, gardens and entryways. Strong consideration should be made towards the installation of a walkway since the curb appeal of your home is what brings buyers through your front door.

Organic Gardens

Organic home gardens have become a growing trend in the United States. With the increasing prices of fresh produce and broad awareness of the chemicals used and quality of the food we buy at the store, organic gardens are popping up in backyards and roof top decks across the country. A turnkey food producing garden has become a favorable trait amongst buyers in today's market place versus paying for food at the chain stores.

The most popular form of home edible gardens are raised garden beds. If you want to create raised garden beds on your property to appeal to this audience, I have provided a basic example of how to do it below:

How to make a raised bed garden

Raised garden beds are great for vegetable and herb gardens, as well as flower gardens. Fruits, such as strawberries, grapes, blueberries, and raspberries, also do very well in a contained raised bed.

To begin, most people use wood to build their raised gardens beds. Some people use concrete blocks or natural stone, but I am going to explain how to do it with wood. Be sure to use regular non-treated wood for your raised garden beds. The downside is that non-treated wood will rot over time, but treated wood will potentially emit chemicals into the dirt which will then get into your food, defeating the purpose of growing your own food.

Below are instructions for building your own wood raised bed garden.

Step one:

Select a well dedicated site in your yard to install the gardening beds. Remember that you are trying to improve your home with functionality and aesthetics. Choose an area that is level and has plenty of light. While choosing the location of your garden, keep in mind that you want the beds located in an area that will look nice and inviting when completed with proper creation of walkways and such.

Step two:

Once you have determined your location, you need to figure out the shape and size of your garden. How many beds will you create, how large will they be and will you have enough room left over to maneuver around the beds for watering and caring for the plants. It is a good idea to keep the planting bed boxes around four feet wide so you can access the middle of the bed from either side. However, when placing your garden bed against a wall or fence, it should be no more than three feet wide. The length of the garden bed will be determined by the amount of space available and how you think it will ultimately look when completed. Six inch tall garden beds are a good start. Vegetables grow well in a bed that is six inches deep so there is no need to go much taller than this. If your soil is hard or bad and you are planning to grow crops that grow deep into the soil like carrots or parsnips then your bed should be at least ten inches deep.

Step three:

Prepare the area for your garden beds. Once you know the size and shape of your bed, you need to clear the area where you will build your beds and begin growing your plants. It is highly suggested that you dig out the existing sod and loosen the soil with a shovel or garden fork before building back up the soil. If you are in a hurry, laying cardboard or newspaper over the existing grass or plants will stop the vegetation beneath the paper and kill it off. You can build up your growing dirt above the paper.

Step four:

Construct the garden bed boxes using your non-treated lumber. Since I suggested 6 inch tall garden beds, you will need to purchase 2 X 6 lumber and cut it to the appropriate size to make your boxes. Attach the pieces together at the corners however you like using galvanized screws or nails.

Step Five:

Now that you have your garden bed boxes made, it is time to fill them with dirt. The point of a raised bed garden is the opportunity to create perfect gardening soil. Fill your bed with a good mixture of quality topsoil, compost, and rotted manure. Once filled and raked level, you are ready to begin planting and gardening.

There is no shortage of magazines on home organic gardens and landscaping. Thumb through books and magazines at your local bookstore and gather ideas on garden beds. Try to determine what will look the best in your backyard and attract the most buyers. My suggestion is to create an area with walkways and a little sitting area to enjoy the garden in the summer. When you stage your home for sale, you can put a little cafe set (table and 2 chairs) amongst your garden beds with a bottle of wine, two glasses and a book on gardening. Build the dream.

Planting Beds

Planting beds are similar to raised planting beds for organic home gardens; however, planting beds can also include flowers, bushes, trees, bird baths and more. Accent your yard with tasteful planting beds finished with dark mulch or beauty bark to give your yard a polished look and enhanced curb appeal.

Planting beds do not have to be raised beds. You are not trying to grow food. Planting beds are spots that don't include grass.

The garden should complement the style of the house. Add vibrant color by planting vines, ornamental grasses and perennials in garden areas. Creating the right look and flow throughout the yard can give you a competitive edge over other homes on the market where less thought was put into the property. As most homeowners do not give a lot of attention to the proper design and flow of their landscape, doing so will give your home value a boost over other homes on the market.

Remove Garbage and Debris from Exterior

Clean up the exterior of your house and make a good first impression:

- Remove and haul away old tree limbs and branches that have fallen into the yard
- Removed broken down cars
- Remove old car tires or car parts
- Clean up old dead leaves that have fallen and are decomposing over the grass
- Remove any garbage and waste that may have blown into the yard
- Remove extra building materials and stone work left behind from household projects
- Remove old landscaping elements that are no longer being used but for some reason are growing moss next to your house
- Lastly, remove anything that does not belong and obstructs a clear view of your home and landscaping.

As soon as the For Sale sign is posted in your front yard, people will immediately begin analyzing and judging every detail of your home as it appears from the street. Put your best foot forward with a clean and tidy property to lure potential buyers.

Remove, Rejuvenate or Replace Old or Broken Patio Furniture

Old patio furniture in the yard can be unsightly. Plastic furniture loses its color while wood furniture rots and falls apart. Any painted furniture will chip and require repainting. Pillows and different sorts of fabric that make up the furniture gets worn, dirty and eventually falls apart.

I repetitively comment about having a polished look in your yard for optimal curb appeal. One of the factors that lends itself to a polished look are items such as outdoor furniture. Furniture in your front yard, back yard, on the patio, deck or porch should be clean and fresh looking. If you can restore the old furniture with a fresh coat of paint and some new cushions, that will make a world of different. If you can afford to spend a bit more, you might be able to replace the furniture for less than $500 to stage your outdoors.

Note: Outdoor furniture does not remain with the house unless it is a permanent fixture. If you are debating how much money to spend on outdoor furniture, remember that it goes with you to your next home unless your buyer negotiates a special deal with you to keep your furniture. With this being said, you can rent outdoor furniture to stage the outdoor living area while you are selling and save further money.

Paint the Neighbors House

I enjoy thinking outside the box. Painting your neighbor's house to improve the appearance of your own is a great example of thinking outside the box. Your home is only as good as your neighbor's home. Nobody wants to live next to an ugly house. And unfortunately, some people (neighbors) do not care about the appearance of their own home. In some cases, your neighbors care about how their home looks, but they cannot afford to do anything about it. Lastly, there are the folks that keep talking about fixing up their house, but never commit to it for personal reasons. Whatever the case, I know people that have offered to have their neighbor's house painted in order to increase the value and curb appeal of their own home. It is a brilliant idea and with all of the competition there is amongst painters in a neighborhood, you might be able to increase the value and appearance of your house dramatically by paying $2500 to paint your neighbors house. If your neighbor agrees to do this, it is a win win for everyone. Your home sells quicker because it is surrounded by nice homes and your neighbor gets a fresh new paint job.

Landscape the Neighbors Yard

Everyone has a neighbor in the neighborhood that lets their grass grow too tall and allows the trees and shrubs to get to overgrown. In many cases, the occupants don't even care and think it's normal. In some cases, the home is a rental property and the renters have no interest in keeping up the appearance of the yard. A simple landscape maintenance could make your neighbor's property look quite a bit nicer in a single day. Living next to an overgrown jungle is not likely desirable for any buyer. It will be a great benefit to somehow persuade your neighbor to clean up their yard or offer to pay a landscaper to clean it up and haul away the yard waste for them. Unfortunately, sometimes the neighbors will not accept your offer because they are satisfied with the way the yard looks or they don't want to be bothered. My father is trying to sell his house and buyers are passing on his home because one of his neighbors has let their property get overgrown with 2 feet tall grass, bushes, intermingled trees, and more. He offered to have their property professionally landscaped and the neighbor told him no thank you. My father will be forced to accept a lower price than he wants to sell his home because buyers don't want to live next door to an overgrown jungle in a residential neighborhood.

Clear Debris from Neighbors Yard

You have seen unsightly yards with garbage, rotting stumps, old car parts, etc. Nobody wants to live next to a trashy property. If you can talk to the neighbor and kindly request that they clean it up because you are selling your home, that would be your best bet. If the neighbor does not want to clean it up, your next step might be to offer to pay to have the junk and debris removed and hauled to the nearest trash dump. If your neighbor is a collector of odd things and likes to put them on display in their front yard, like the toilet planter, then there is not much you can do to change them. To your neighbor, the items in their yard are not junk, it is art. If you can get your neighbors property looking good, it will help increase the value and salability of your home.

Create Greenhouse

A greenhouse is a glass enclosed garden plot. A garden from which you have choice flowers, fruits and vegetables in and out of season, all year round. You can control the humidity, moisture, temperature and spread of insects.

As you know, every buyer is different and not every feature of your house appeals to every potential buyer the same way. We typically suggest that you choose the most popular and universal improvements to obtain the best return on your investment. A green house can make a nice improvement to your house. However, not everyone cares about gardening or finding a house with a greenhouse. In fact, a lot of people will not care whether you have a greenhouse or not. While a nice greenhouse would improve your home, it would fall towards the bottom of the list of improvements suggested to improve your home because the cost can be significant to build a nice one and you may not appeal to any more buyers than you already are. As people are becoming more and more food conscious (pesticides in food, increasing prices, etc.), they are growing more food and herbs at home. Greenhouses will become increasingly popular as well, just as outdoor raised gardening beds have become very popular lately in urban and high density neighborhoods.

Add Workshop, Artist Studio or Playhouse

Adding an outbuilding can attract buyers. First you must determine what type of an outbuilding would best suit the house and the neighborhood. For example, in a blue collar neighborhood a workshop with electricity may be a valuable addition to the property to attract the hobbyist, metal worker or auto mechanic seeking a special building to take on outdoor projects. In some instances, such as closer to the city, an artist studio may be more attractive to the buyer that is an avid painter or creator and needs a space outside of the house to enjoy their art or musical activities. Lastly is the playhouse. A playhouse is a great addition to a home to attract buyers in a family neighborhood. When the kids are excited about a house, it can make parents/buyers excited about a home. A playhouse for children does not have to be a large outbuilding. In fact it can be quite small with one door and a window. If done well, a playhouse makes a wonderful compliment to a backyard garden.

Adding a workshop or studio outbuilding will cost $10,000 - $20,000 to do well enough to add value to your home. Once completed with a floor, drywall and electric, you will have created an additional useable space that is sure to increase the value of your home and attract buyers.

Add Jungle Gym Feature to Attract Families

A jungle gym feature in your backyard can definitely be an improvement to your home depending upon who your target audience is. For example, if you are in a family neighborhood and your buyers will most likely have children, then a jungle gym feature will definitely attract buyers. However, if you live in a mixed neighborhood and your buyer could be anyone from a single person to a family, then it may not be a feature worth installing on the property, as it could be seen as a nuisance to a potential buyer with no family. With this being said a jungle gym / swing set can either be a benefit to your value or detract from the value depending upon where you live. Know your audience and make your decision wisely.

Jungle gym features are available in a variety of packages. A jungle gym feature can be a simple swing set with a slide, a little house, or a full on play structure with swings, fort, playhouse and slide all in one. The price can vary from $300 up to $4000 and greater depending upon how elaborate a system you choose. If you decide that according to your demographic, it would be smart to install a jungle gym feature, do not install one that is too large and over shadows the backyard. Even though you are appealing to children and families, the parents or those children will still want to enjoy the backyard as well. If you fill up the backyard with a huge jungle gym, the backyard becomes too one-sided towards children and less desirable for the adults/people with the money.

Pave, Repave or Pour New Concrete Driveway

If you have a cement driveway that is deteriorating away in large chunks, you may want to consider replacing the broken slabs. The good think about concrete driveways is that they are very sturdy and hardly ever fail. When they do fail, they are divided up into large sections as opposed to one solid piece of concrete so you don't have to replace the entire driveway to make it look new again. You can pick and choose the worst sections to replace. Unfortunately, having new concrete poured is not cheap. Pouring concrete is not something I recommend you try to take on yourself because it takes a large amount of concrete to fill a small space and then you need to know how to smooth it over with the perfect texture like the professionals. If you have small cracks in your concrete driveway, this is probably of no concern to you. However, if you have slabs that are split and tilted different directions due to the ground settling beneath the driveway, or roots jamming the concrete upwards, you should highly consider correcting this. If a potential buyer is bouncing in their seat as they drive up your driveway, then you are making a bad first impression.

Topcoat Driveway (Blacktop)

A fresh coat of blacktop or sealant over your weathered asphalt driveway is a quick and affordable way to polish up the exterior of your home while preserving an important feature of your home. Whether you do this yourself or hire a local business to seal your driveway, the results can be astonishing.

If you decide to do this yourself, there are a few basic things you should know. In order to properly seal the driveway, you must first seal all of the cracks with a tar crack filler. This product as well as the sealant is very sticky and will ruin any clothing and shoes that it comes into contact with. Be sure to wear some old clothes or protect your clothing and boots with the painters coveralls you get at the hardware store. Once you have sealed your cracks, you can apply the black sealant over the driveway. Determine the square footage of your driveway by multiplying the width and length of your driveway. Head to your local home improvement store and purchase the appropriate amount of sealant and tools necessary to apply the sealant to your driveway. The sealant is typically applied by a large flat broom and you just spread it on. Once the entire driveway is sealed, it should take a few days to dry and you are done.

The cost to have a local company seal your driveway may not cost much more than the cost of your supplies, so if you have a little bit extra spending money for this project, I recommend you get some bids and avoid a sticky situation.

Add a Garage

If your home does not have a garage, but you have the land space to build one, you may want to consider building one. The second biggest expense for consumers (aside from houses) is their automobiles and they want to protect them any way they can.

A garage creates a space to protect automobiles from the elements that damage them and theft. In addition, a garage is a great place to store yard equipment, garbage cans, tools and carry on projects. The list of possibilities is endless with a garage.

Building a garage is no easy task and can be quite expensive. Building a garage is not something I can easily explain in one paragraph, but I can say that there are ways to cut costs. You can purchase pre-fabricated garages. I don't personally like the look of them, but you can order fully functional garages with single bays or double bays. These prefabricated garages come in metal or wood. In fact, if you really want to save money, you can purchase a prefabricated garage to be built onsite and pour your garage floor at another time. The garage will add so much value on its own that a gravel garage floor will be good enough to invoke a sale. Adding a garage is definitely something to consider if you have the space and the finances.

Improve Garage Interior with Drywall & Paint

Most garage walls and ceilings are an afterthought to builders. Most builders or homeowners leave the walls bare and unfinished. Sometimes builders will drywall the walls and ceiling, but they do put a final coat of mud on the seams, sand and paint. If you feel like your potential buyer might appreciate a cleaner look in the garage then you should spruce up the garage to accommodate. Many people will value a garage with finished ceiling and walls. A finished garage can be a great place to work on projects, hobbies, create art or store a high-end car.

In most cases, people will not care too much how the garage looks so this improvement to your home will not yield a high return. If your house is small, a buyer may appreciate the additional living space potential of your garage once you show the garage all cleaned up. Finishing the walls with drywall and paint will get your buyers thinking that they have more livable space than they actually are getting. And if you live in a neighborhood that attracts owners of nice vehicles, then you have more incentive to polish up interior of the garage to create the perfect showroom for a vintage or expensive automobile that some buyers may have.

The cost of this improvement will vary greatly depending upon whether you have to have drywall hung, taped, mudded, then painted. As opposed to if your drywall is already hung and you just need it finished and painted. The cost can range from $500 - $2500 depending on these factors. You may learn that the return on investment may not be worth the expense.

Add Shelving & Storage Systems to Garage

A garage is not complete without shelving and storage for tools and other outdoor items. Most garages have some sort of shelving or peg-board with hooks to hang some tools. The question is, can you make the garage shelving and tool storage even better?

Home improvement stores carry a variety of storage options from wire shelving systems to rolling tool cabinets that securely lock.

Shelving:

Shelving comes in different lengths, strengths and prices. The less expensive shelving types will not hold much weight, nor do they look very nice. The least expensive shelving type is the white wire shelving. Some other types of metal shelving are thicker chrome shelving or sheet metal shelving that you painstakingly screw together piece by piece. One of my favorite types of wire shelving that I purchased was a 3 shelf steel collapsible shelving unit. It was a four feet wide storage rack on wheels that came in a flat box. It was already built, but collapsed in the box. All I had to do was open up the box, unfold the shelving system like an accordion and hook two hooks into place so the shelving system would not collapse. For the price it was completely worth it because I didn't have to build anything and the result was a great looking shelving system that I could roll around my garage as needed. A few of these shelving units could quickly add storage to any garage.

As you dig deeper into this, you will find isles full of shelving and storage ideas at your local hardware or home improvement store.

Storage cabinets

Storage cabinets are a step up from shelving because they offer two things shelves don't: You can hide your stored items and you can lock them up securely.

Home improvement stores typically have a couple models of storage cabinets depending on your price point. The less expensive storage cabinets usually don't look good and are constructed of particle board which will eventually break apart or easily damaged by moisture. You can purchase cabinets that are the same height as kitchen cabinets or cabinets as tall as an armoire for storing more things. The kitchen cabinet height cabinets are great for creating space for storage, while also creating a work bench situation. The cabinets usually have drawers which are nice for storing all of your tools for easy access. The taller cabinets will hold your paint, cleaning supplies, sporting goods, outdoor tools, fertilizer, insect repellents and more.

On the higher end of the garage cabinetry you start finding cabinets reinforced with or made completely of metal. These cabinets will be more solid and offer more protection over your tools as opposed to the less expensive particle board cabinets. The cabinets will cost considerably more, but if you only need 3-4 cabinets, the cost may be worth it. A row of low and tall cabinets makes a garage look really sharp.

The last piece of advice I can give on garage cabinets is to try and find cabinets with wheels. The cheaper brands may not have wheels on them. Wheels are great if you want to roll the cabinets around and clean the floors every once in a while. The cabinets will get very heavy with all of your household items in them. You don't want to have to unpack them every time you need to move the cabinets. It is best to have wheels beneath them. If you find cabinets that you like at the store, but they don't have wheels on them, you can always buy casters from the same store and screw them onto the bottoms of the cabinets yourself.

Take the opportunity to create a showcase garage with plenty of shelving and storage cabinets. A clean tidy garage will lots of custom storage options will impress any home buyer.

Finish 2nd Floor Storage Area in Garage

If you have a garage with an exposed pitched roof in it, you should consider turning that empty space above your head into useable storage space. I don't necessarily mean that you need to drywall and paint the walls and ceiling and install a stairwell. Creating useable storage space can be as simple as installing plywood sheeting (flooring) along the floor joists (you may want to add floor joists for added strength and support since the existing joists probably were not installed with the intention of supporting a floor). Once you have a solid floor installed, you need to create a way to get up to the floor.

An easy way to do this is by purchasing a pull down staircase/ladder which you can purchase from a home improvement store. Pull down attic ladders / stairways cost anywhere from $200 - $300 and can be installed by the homeowner or a handyman. Once you have a floor and a stairway or ladder to access the upper floor, you have just created a wonderful useable storage space that will attract buyers. The final suggestion I have regarding this new useable storage space would be a light. If you have electricity running to the garage, be sure to capitalize on that and install a light in the upper part of your garage to make the storage space more functional and attractive.

Pour Concrete Floor in Garage

Is your garage concrete floor worn-out, stained, uneven, or cracked concrete garage floor? This will happen with age. The ground settles, tree roots grow beneath your garage, salt drips off of cars in the winter eating holes in the concrete and oil drips out of most cars. The garage floor can be victim to the harshest substances, including oils, salt, acids, and paints. Most garage floors are made of concrete, which is a semi-porous material and acts like a sponge absorbing small amounts of liquid material dropped or spilled on it.

The liquids that are spilled onto the concrete floor permeate the surface and stay on the layer just below the surface. This is why you see so many stains on concrete floors that are next to impossible to eliminate. Over the years, the floor takes a beating and can look pretty unsightly. If patching the floor does not do the trick any more, then it might be time to have a new garage floor poured.

A concrete company can remove your old garage floor and pour a brand-new floor for your garage that will make you proud and improve the value of your home.

A new concrete floor goes through a curing process that lasts about 7-10 days. A concrete company will recommend sealing your new concrete garage floor to protect it from all of the damaging elements: oil, paint and dirt or salt from car tires from permeating the cement floor.

In the end, if your garage floor is a disaster area, it makes use of the garage less desirable and actually lowers the value of your home. Imagine trying to sell a home with a horrible garage floor. It can be embarrassing and will continue getting worse over time. Prices to pour a new concrete floor will vary. Be sure to get multiple bids and references from local contractors.

Upgrade Garage Door

If you currently have unsightly garage doors, or maybe garage doors that are functional, but are not consistent with the style of your home, consider replacing them with brand new doors. Garage doors come in a variety of styles to match any type of home whether it be classic or contemporary. You can get a large single bay door or matching double doors. You have options for glass window panes (frosted or clear). Another improvement to garage doors is to convert two small garage doors into one large garage door so you can fit larger vehicles into the garage. Older homes had small driveways and small garage doors. I don't really understand this since old cars seem huge to me.

If you begin shopping for new garage doors, prepare for some decision making because there are a lot of great options available. You will be choosing between different styles, materials, colors and prices. Choose wisely beginning with a style that coincides with the style of your home. In a situation like there where you could be overwhelmed by choices, begin with your budget to limit your choices and then decide which style of door(s) will work best to showcase your home in the greatest light.

Install an Automatic Garage Door Opener

If your garage doors do not have automatic garage door openers on them, you may want to consider this improvement. Garage doors can be heavy and cumbersome to lift and lower manually. If you can fit a car in your garage and the door is not automatic, you should definitely consider purchasing and installing a garage door opener. Most people will not want to pull into their driveway, get out of the car, open the garage door, get back into their car, pull into the garage, park, then shut the door. Even with garages that are too small for cars, an automatic garage door is handy for loading bicycles in and out, motorcycles, lawn equipment and more.

Convert a Garage into Living Space

If you can obtain the proper permits and it is allowable through your local code enforcement, a garage conversion to living space can dramatically increase the value of your home while increasing square footage. A family may appreciate a your home with the extra bedroom, master bath, recreation room or second living room that you created out of the single or double car garage attached to your home. I have seen many great conversions of garages. If you can obtain the permits for it, depending upon where your home is, a garage may be converted into multiple types of spaces: Addition to house, art studio, mother-in-law apartment, rental unit or more. The opportunities are endless. For an attached garage, you probably would only want to consider the options above relating to the additional square footage in the form of an extra bedroom or living space. However, if you are converting a detached garage into livable space, your options are different. You would not create an additional bathroom or bedroom in a detached garage, however, I have seen people create wonderful artist studios and workshops. My favorite conversion is into rentable space in high density neighborhoods. Creating an income producing unit on your property increases the value of your property and also expands the number of buyers that can afford your house. If the price of your house was once out of range for many buyers, the addition of an income producing remodeled garage into an apartment could bring in enough income to fill the gap between a payment that a buyer once couldn't afford. With this additional rental property on your land, you have made your house more affordable because buyers will have the potential to offset some of the mortgage with rental income.

Converting a garage into livable space is a great idea to attract more buyers as long as you still have some sort of parking on your property for vehicles. Converting a garage into another type of space may not be such a good idea if it means people have to park on the street.

Converting a garage to a livable space will not be cheap. It will easily cost over $10,000. However, since you will not be dealing with appliances, tile and granite, your costs will mostly be wrapped up in permits, insulation, drywall, carpet and some doors or windows if you don't already have nice ones in the garage.

Section 3

Special Table of Contents

Improvements categorized by Interior, Exterior, Cost & ROI

The following tables consist of different variations of all the home improvements described within this book. I divided the improvements up into two main categories:

- Table 1: Indoor Improvements
- Table 2: Exterior Improvements.

Within each category, you will find three subcategories:

- Expensive Improvements
- Mid-Level Improvements ($2500-$10,000)
- Inexpensive Improvements ($2499 and under).

I then divided these subcategories up based upon the return on investment for each. Return on investment can be defined as the percentage increase in value per dollar spent on an improvement.

Using the following charts I created for you, you can create your own improvement plan on your home to best match your needs and approximate budget. Choose from the list expensive to inexpensive improvements to improve your home. Your final list may consist of some ideas that hardly cost anything along with a few improvements that cost a sizeable amount but offer you a high return.

The last table number 4 is a blank improvement chart for you to use to map out your own home improvement plan. Choose a combination of Indoor and Exterior improvements with a mix of expensive, moderately priced and inexpensive improvements that all have a positive return on investment. The improvements you choose will be based upon your budget and skill level if doing things yourself. The final improvement list you create should serve as a great tool to help guide you to selling your house at the highest price possible.

*You will see the same improvement showing up in multiple price points because the cost of the improvements can vary depending on the size and scope of your project. Many improvements have variations that will affect the cost such as type of materials, finishes, etc. (a cheapest, c expensive).

Table 1a: Indoor Improvements – Expensive ($8,000+)

High Return on Investment

- ☐ Complete Kitchen remodel: flooring, cabinets, plumbing fixtures, countertops, lighting
- ☐ Large Dormer Master Bedroom
- ☐ Add master bath to bedroom
- ☐ Update the kitchen Cabinets: Reface or Replace
- ☐ Add a Bathroom
- ☐ Add an Extension to Your Home
- ☐ Create a Large Dormer
- ☐ Convert the Unfinished Basement into Livable Space

Moderate Return on Investment

- ☐ Complete Bath Remodel: Flooring, Bath Fixtures, Vanity, Lighting and other Amenities.
- ☐ Plumbing: Complete Replacement
- ☐ Electrical: Complete Replacement
- ☐ Create Rentable Space: Income Producing Mother-In-Law Unit
- ☐ Add a Sunroom

Low Return on Investment

- ☐ Convert a Bedroom into a Bathroom
- ☐ Create a Master Bedroom
- ☐ Heat: Change Entire Heating System from one type to an Improved System
- ☐ Go green: Eco-friendly Homes Bring in a Higher Value

Table 1b: Indoor Improvements – Mid-Level ($2000-$7,999)

High Return on Investment

☐ Update the kitchen Cabinets: Paint, Refinish, Reface or Replace

☐ Update Kitchen Countertops (w/stone)

☐ Improve Kitchen Lighting (high end lighting Including Recessed, Under-Cabinet and More)

☐ Custom Built Kitchen Island

☐ Upgrade Appliances with High-End Appliances

☐ Upgrade Kitchen Flooring to tile or stone

☐ Level House Out (w/limited access)

☐ Repaint Entire Interior

☐ Upgrade Lighting throughout Home

☐ Flooring: Replace Old Floor Coverings with New/Updated Flooring

☐ Deferred Maintenance (large scale)

☐ Refinish Hardwood Floors in lieu of Replacement

☐ Remove Walls to Expand Space

☐ Convert the Partially Finished Basement into Livable Space

Moderate Return on Investment

☐ Create a Breakfast Nook Area

☐ Add a Kitchen Pantry

- ☐ Bathtub & Shower Resurfacing
- ☐ Upgrade Bath Flooring (replacing with stone or tile flooring)
- ☐ Dormer Master Bedroom (Small dormer)
- ☐ Complete Master Bedroom Remodel
- ☐ Plumbing: Repair and/or Replace Sections
- ☐ Electrical: Repair and/or Replace Sections
- ☐ Coved Ceilings
- ☐ Create a Sunroom (using existing space)
- ☐ Create a Dormer
- ☐ Insulate the Home (with limited access)
- ☐ Heat: Upgrade Heating System to More Efficient System
- ☐ Heat: Change Entire Heating System from one type to an Improved System
- ☐ Tankless Water Heater
- ☐ Complete Low Voltage Wiring for Phone, Cable & Internet Combined
- ☐ Install Skylights (multiple)
- ☐ Create Rentable Space: Income Producing Mother-In-Law Unit

Low Return on Investment

- ☐ Add a Jacuzzi Tub to Bathroom
- ☐ Convert a Bedroom into Bathroom
- ☐ Add a Laundry Room on Same Level of Master

- ☐ Go green: Eco-friendly Homes Bring in a Higher Value
- ☐ Create a Master Bedroom
- ☐ Vaulted Ceilings / Exposed Beams
- ☐ Install Fireplace
- ☐ Upgrade Fireplace
- ☐ State of the art Audio and Sound
- ☐ Add Air Conditioning / Central Air
- ☐ Turn crawl Space Into Useable Space
- ☐ Add an Entertainment Bar

Table 1c: Indoor Improvements – Inexpensive ($0-$1999)

High Return on Investment

- ☐ Update the Kitchen Cabinets: Paint, Refinish
- ☐ Update Kitchen Countertops
- ☐ Improve Kitchen Lighting
- ☐ Upgrade Plumbing Fixtures in the Kitchen
- ☐ Paint the Kitchen
- ☐ Install Under-Cabinet Lighting in Kitchen
- ☐ Upgrade Bath Flooring (good quality new vinyl or Tile for Small Bath <$2k)
- ☐ Shower: Replace Shower Curtains with Glass Doors
- ☐ Replace Old Bath Fixtures with New Ones
- ☐ New Bath Vanity
- ☐ Replace Towel Bars in Bath
- ☐ Get Rid of Mold and Mildew in the Bathrooms and Kitchen
- ☐ Paint Master Bedroom
- ☐ Level House Out (w/easy access)
- ☐ Clean Windows Inside and Out
- ☐ Repair Holes and Cracks in Plaster and Drywall throughout
- ☐ Texture Coated Ceilings: remove texture or cover with drywall

- [ ] Install or Replace Baseboard Trim
- [ ] Install or Replace Window Trim
- [ ] Add Interior Trim & Millwork (to homes without)
- [ ] Paint Important Rooms
- [ ] Upgrade Lighting
- [ ] Flooring: Replace Old Floor Coverings with New/Updated Flooring (moderate grade materials)
- [ ] Interior Design with a Professional
- [ ] Increase the Visual Square Feet of Your Home
- [ ] Bring the Outdoors In
- [ ] Make it Brighter
- [ ] Make Sure Every Light Bulb in the Home Works
- [ ] Deferred Maintenance (small scale)
- [ ] Deep Clean your House
- [ ] Remove or Control Odors
- [ ] Refinish Hardwood Floors in lieu of Replacement
- [ ] Remove Walls to Expand Space (single wall)
- [ ] Wall coverings: Update or Remove and Paint
- [ ] Repair Old Windows
- [ ] Change out Window Hardware
- [ ] Replace Door Knobs, Hinges and Cabinet Pulls throughout and Where Needed
- [ ] De-clutter: Remove Garbage and Debris from Interior Finished Storage Spaces
- [ ] Turn Crawl Space into Useable Space

Moderate Return on Investment

- ☐ Kitchen Island (store bought island)
- ☐ Create a Breakfast Nook Area (space already exists)
- ☐ Add a Kitchen Pantry (Space already exists)
- ☐ Bathroom Porcelain Refinishing
- ☐ Add Built-Ins to Bedroom Closets
- ☐ Complete Master Bedroom Remodel
- ☐ Plumbing Repair
- ☐ Electrical Repair
- ☐ Upgrade Electrical Panel
- ☐ Obtain Planning Permission on Prior Improvements
- ☐ Insulate the Home (if easily accessible)
- ☐ Programmable Thermostats
- ☐ Tankless Water Heater (small heaters)
- ☐ Go green: Eco-friendly Homes Bring in a Higher Value
- ☐ Complete Low Voltage Wiring for Phone, Cable & Internet Combined
- ☐ Install Solar Tubes
- ☐ Install Single Skylight
- ☐ Clear out Unfinished Crawl Spaces

Low Return on Investment

- ☐ Add Railings to Stairwells
- ☐ Add Smoke Detectors
- ☐ Install a Security System

- ☐ Replace or Install Window Coverings
- ☐ Coved Ceilings
- ☐ Archways & Architectural Improvement
- ☐ Install Updated Light Switch and Outlet Covers throughout Your Home
- ☐ Install Updated Light Switches and/or Dimmers
- ☐ Vaulted Ceilings / Exposed Beams
- ☐ Install or Replace Your Doorbell
- ☐ Weather-stripping
- ☐ Change the Filter in Your Air Conditioner
- ☐ Professionally Hardwire Your Home for Telephone
- ☐ Professionally Hardwire Your Home for Cable Television
- ☐ Professionally Hardwire Your Home for Internet
- ☐ State of the art Audio and Sound
- ☐ Ceiling Fans
- ☐ Add a water filtration System
- ☐ Add an Entertainment Bar

Table 2a: Exterior Improvements – Expensive ($8,000+)

High Return on Investment

- ☐ Paint Exterior (Large Home or requiring lots of restoration)
- ☐ Build a Deck (Large Deck)
- ☐ Replace Roof
- ☐ Replace All windows
- ☐ Siding Replacement
- ☐ Install Solar Energy Panels
- ☐ Pave, Repave or Pour New Concrete Driveway
- ☐ Add a Garage

Moderate Return on Investment

- ☐ Install Eves
- ☐ Install Soffits
- ☐ Upgrade Drainage System: Sewer Line
- ☐ Make your home Flood Proof: Exterior or Interior French Drain w/Sump Pump
- ☐ Install Swimming Pool or Lap Pool
- ☐ Convert a Garage into Living Space

Low Return on Investment

- ☐ Add a Hot Tub
- ☐ Add Workshop, Artist Studio or Playhouse

Table 2b: Exterior Improvements – Mid-Level ($2000-$7,999)

High Return on Investment

- ☐ Paint Exterior (Average Home)
- ☐ Build a Deck (Average Size Deck)
- ☐ Repair or Replace Roof
- ☐ Replace Rotted Wood (large amounts)
- ☐ Replace or Repair Porch Flooring
- ☐ Replace or Upgrade Porch Railings
- ☐ Make Your Home Flood Proof: Exterior or Interior French Drain w/Sump Pump
- ☐ Add Exterior Trim
- ☐ Install Fence
- ☐ Repaint Fences and Trellis Outside
- ☐ Create Privacy
- ☐ Pave, Repave or Pour New Concrete Driveway

Moderate Return on Investment

- ☐ Improve Eves
- ☐ Improve Soffits
- ☐ Replace Some Windows
- ☐ Add Windows for more Light
- ☐ Exterior / Outdoor Landscape Lighting
- ☐ Add Sprinkler System (Professional Installation)

- [ ] Install Walkways
- [ ] Install Water Feature
- [ ] Install Stone Patio
- [ ] Paint the Neighbors House
- [ ] Upgrade Garage Door

Low Return on Investment

- [ ] Install Shutter and Window Box Sets that Match
- [ ] Add a Hot Tub
- [ ] Rejuvenate or Replace old or Broken Patio Furniture
- [ ] Create Greenhouse
- [ ] Add Workshop, Artist Studio or Playhouse
- [ ] Add Jungle Gym Feature to Attract Families
- [ ] Pour Concrete Floor in Garage
- [ ] Convert a Garage into Living Space

Table 2c: Exterior Improvements – Inexpensive ($0-$1999)

High Return on Investment

- ☐ Build a Deck (small deck)
- ☐ Refinish Deck and Seal with Tinted Color
- ☐ Repair or Patch Roof
- ☐ Clean the Roof of Debris
- ☐ Repair Siding
- ☐ Replace Window Replace
- ☐ Rotted Wood (In spaces with easy access)
- ☐ Replace Front Door
- ☐ Paint Front Door
- ☐ Repair & Paint Porch flooring
- ☐ Repair & Paint Porch Railings
- ☐ Power Wash the Exterior of your Home
- ☐ Add Exterior Trim
- ☐ Full Green Lawn: Sod, Seed or Weed
- ☐ Keep Lawn Well Mowed
- ☐ Repaint Fences and Trellis Outside
- ☐ Create Privacy
- ☐ Remove Unwanted Trees and Shrubs
- ☐ Landscape Cleanup
- ☐ Remove Garbage and Debris from Exterior

- ☐ Landscape the Neighbors Yard
- ☐ Clear Debris from Neighbors Yard

Moderate Return on Investment

- ☐ Repair or Install New Gutters
- ☐ Replace Cracked Window Panes
- ☐ Exterior / Outdoor Landscape Lighting
- ☐ Add Sprinkler System (do-it-yourself)
- ☐ Add Electrical Receptacles Outdoors
- ☐ Add Outdoor Faucets
- ☐ Insulate all Exposed Pipes
- ☐ Street Numbers
- ☐ New Mailbox
- ☐ House Numbers
- ☐ Small Fence
- ☐ Install Small Water Feature
- ☐ Install Small Stone Patio
- ☐ Add Shelving & Storage Systems to Garage
- ☐ Upgrade Garage Door
- ☐ Install an Automatic Garage Door Opener

Low Return on Investment

- ☐ Install Rain Barrel
- ☐ Add a Window for More Light
- ☐ Add or Remove Screen Door: (keeps out insects, but does it take away from curb appeal?)

- ☐ Test and/or Repair all Outdoor Drains to Prevent Flooding
- ☐ Create a Rock Garden (Do-it-yourself)
- ☐ Install Walkways (lower cost materials)
- ☐ Organic Gardens
- ☐ Planting Beds
- ☐ Remove, Rejuvenate or Replace Old or Broken Patio Furniture
- ☐ Add Jungle Gym Feature to Attract Families
- ☐ Improve Garage Interior with Drywall & Paint
- ☐ Finish 2nd Floor Storage Area in Garage
- ☐ Convert a Garage into Living Space

Table 3: Create Your Own Improvement Plan

Now that you have been given a multitude of ways to improve the value of your home it is time to put some of these ideas into action.

On the following page, I created a chart for you to write down the improvements you wish to make along with their approximate costs in accordance with your budget. Your budget equals the amount of cash you are willing to invest on improvements to your home in order to increase the value of your home in hopes of selling for the highest price possible.

In the last two sections, I broke down the different improvements based on approximate price and return on investment.

To begin your plan, start by inputting your budget at the bottom of the chart. Once you have written down your budget, choose the improvements you want to make based on price and return, both inside and outside the home. Input those improvements on the chart with the approximate dollar value next to the improvement. The dollar range of my improvements is large, so if you know that you can do something for free or for a particular amount, go ahead and input that amount on the document. Continue to add and delete improvements until you have a plan in which the cost equals or is less than the dollar amount you input for your budget.

I hope you have inspirational ideas to improve the value of your home. I wish you the best of luck in getting the most money out of your home by using some of the ideas in this book.

Your Home Improvement Plan

Interior   **Estimated Cost**

Expensive Improvements

_____   _____

_____   _____

_____   _____

Mid-Level Improvements

_____   _____

_____   _____

_____   _____

Inexpensive Improvements

_____   _____

_____   _____

_____   _____

Exterior

Expensive Improvements

_____   _____

_____   _____

_____   _____

Mid-Level Improvements

_____   _____

_____   _____

_____   _____

Inexpensive Improvements

_____   _____

_____   _____

_____   _____

Your Budget: _____   Estimated Cost: _____

www.ingramcontent.com/pod-product-compliance
Lightning Source LLC
Chambersburg PA
CBHW031928190326
41519CB00007B/451